D1616169

Stuart Library
of Western Americana
University of
the Pacific
Stockton,
California

TO THE SANDWICH ISLANDS ON H.M.S. *BLONDE*

ROBERT DAMPIER (self-portrait)
"A man who lived in . . . spacious days"

TO THE SANDWICH ISLANDS ON H.M.S. *BLONDE*

ROBERT DAMPIER

edited by
PAULINE KING JOERGER

THE UNIVERSITY PRESS OF HAWAII
For Friends of the Library of Hawaii
HONOLULU 1971

Library of Congress Catalog Card Number 73-147156

(formerly University of Hawaii Press, ISBN 0-87022-176-0)

Manufactured in the United States of America

CONTENTS

Dampier, Robert, 1800–1874.
To the Sandwich Islands on H. M. S. Blonde [by] Robert Dampier. Edited by Pauline King Joerger. Honolulu, University Press of Hawaii for Friends of the Library of Hawaii, 1971.

x, 131 p. illus. 23 x 28 cm.

Includes bibliographical references.

1. Blonde (Ship) 2. Voyages and travels. 3. Hawaii—Description and travel—To 1950. I. Joerger, Pauline King, ed. II. Title.

G463.D273 910'.45'0924 [B] 73-147156
ISBN 0-87022-176-0 MARC

Library of Congress 72 [4]

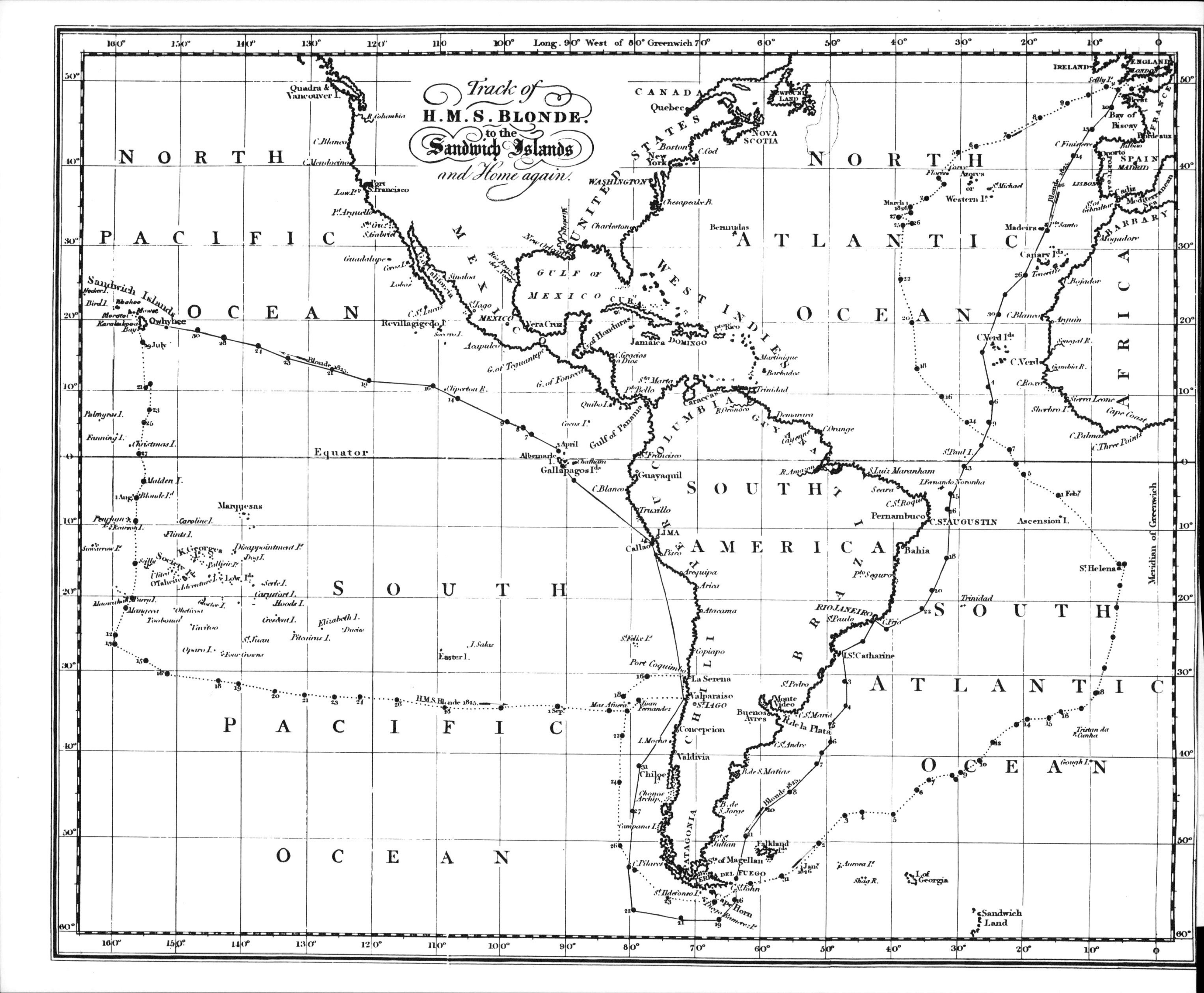

Track of
H.M.S. BLONDE.
to the
Sandwich Islands
and Home again.
Long. 90° West of 80° Greenwich 70°
NORTH PACIFIC OCEAN
NORTH ATLANTIC OCEAN
SOUTH PACIFIC OCEAN
SOUTH ATLANTIC OCEAN
SOUTH AMERICA
CANADA
UNITED STATES
MEXICO
GULF OF MEXICO
WEST INDIES
COLUMBIA
GUYANA
BRAZIL
PERU
CHILI
PATAGONIA
AFRICA
BARBARY
SPAIN
FRANCE
ENGLAND
IRELAND
Sandwich Islands
Owhyhee
Equator
Marquesas
Society Is.
Gallapagos Ids.
Lima
Callao
Valparaiso
Concepcion
Valdivia
Chiloe
Cape Horn
Falkland Ids.
Rio Janeiro
Bahia
Pernambuco
Buenos Ayres
Monte Video
St. Helena
Ascension I.
Tristan da Cunha
Sandwich Land
I. of Georgia
Madeira
Canary Ids.
C. Verd Ids.
Azores or Western Is.
Bermudas
Meridian of Greenwich

INTRODUCTION

In 1825 a young Englishman, Robert Dampier, sailed through the eastern Pacific and kept a journal of his observations. He was twenty-four years old and had lived for the previous six years in Rio de Janeiro. Exuberant, eager to see new parts of the world, he accepted the invitation of George Anson Byron (the poet's cousin), baron, and captain in the British Royal Navy, to serve as artist and draftsman aboard H.M.S. *Blonde* on its assignment to the Hawaiian Islands from England. Late in 1824 he joined the ship at Rio de Janeiro and remained throughout its voyage around Cape Horn, up the western coast of South America, to the Galápagos Islands, the Sandwich (Hawaiian) Islands, and Mauke in the Cook Islands and its return to South America, around the Horn to the island of St. Helena, and finally, in early 1826, to England.

The *Blonde* was sent by the British government to Hawaii to return the bodies of King Kamehameha II (Liholiho) and his favorite queen, Kamamalu. The royal couple had traveled to England with a suite of about ten chiefs and retainers in 1823–1824. In London, the Hawaiian party had been exposed to measles. Kamamalu died of the disease on July 8, 1824, and the king died six days later. King George IV, at the suggestion of his secretary of state for foreign affairs, George Canning, ordered a ship of war to be sent to return the bodies of the royal couple and their suite to the Islands.

Liholiho had undertaken his voyage partly to discuss the idea of a protectorate by Great Britain over the Hawaiian Islands. After his king's death, Boki, governor of Oahu and ranking chief in the party, discussed the proposal with King George and some of his ministers. At that meeting the British monarch agreed that Great Britain would protect the Hawaiian Islands from external dangers but would not concern itself with internal matters. Lord Byron was given command of the mission, with secret instructions to investigate the political situation in Hawaii. He was to avoid involving Great Britain too closely in the affairs of the Hawaiian Kingdom unless internal political instability or external threat seemed to indicate the government's collapse. Then, Byron was to annex the Islands in the name of Great Britain. The mission was a complete success, and Byron made a lasting impression in the Islands, favorable to Britain without committing his government to any responsibility for local Hawaiian affairs.

Robert Dampier held an enviable position aboard the *Blonde*. As artist and draftsman, he sketched landscapes and painted portraits, apparently selecting his subjects by no other standard than his own tastes. He seems not to have had any arduous duties to perform and was free to undertake side trips of his own choosing. Lord Byron often invited him on excursions and to official meetings. At Callao Dampier witnessed a skirmish between Spanish and patriot forces. In Hawaii he conversed with, and observed, most of the important chiefs and chiefesses. In Chile he associated with the aristocracy and knew the patriot leaders of the new nation.

He saw areas seen by few other Westerners of his period. The Pacific traveler rarely visited Mauke; descriptions of its missionary settlement are few. Although Hawaii was on a major trade route between the Pacific Northwest and Asia, the Islands were infrequently visited by literate Westerners. Dampier's journal, then, simply by virtue of its existence, is a valuable addition to the history of the eastern Pacific.

But there is more to the journal. That part which concerns Hawaii is most important. Dampier's descriptions of the Hawaiian chiefs, their personalities and attitudes, add significantly to the scanty material now available. The haughty behavior of Ka'ahumanu, widow of Kamehameha I, emerges powerfully in Dampier's recital of her conduct aboard the *Blonde* and in Hilo as the patron of Lord Byron and his crew. Also significant are his accounts which indicate the impact of Western and Pacific cultures upon one another. For instance, the force of change can be seen in Dampier's depiction of the funeral procession for Liholiho and Kamamalu in Honolulu in which Polynesian and Western rituals were combined in a new pattern neither traditionally Hawaiian nor contemporarily European.

The visits to southwestern South America were sources of important accounts in the journal. There are word sketches of the pleasant life of the upper classes, of Indian chiefs and people at home or at festivities, and of the silver mining around Serena, Chile. Dampier described the Galápagos Islands and its animal life two decades before Charles Darwin arrived aboard the *Beagle*.

Dampier was at his best when describing: the look of things, scenery, and the differing modes of living. He was interested in the looming Andes Mountains, the belching fires of Kilauea volcano, and the black lava ledges of the Galápagos covered with monstrous iguanas. His attention was caught by the design of canoes, the drape of a Spanish mantilla or a Hawaiian *kapa* skirt, and by the possessions and table fare of his hosts.

He was, of course, influenced in his observations by the preconceptions and assumptions of his origins. His criterion was the England of the gentry: the country village, the country gentleman in his perfectly planned park, the "well regulated house, respectful servants, adjoining delightful grounds." The England of the slum dweller, of squalor and disorder, was outside his purview.

He was traveling either in countries that were frontiers of civilization, or in primitive lands where people lived lives totally alien to his, or in regions where nature existed in raw and brutal form. In consequence he was, at times, severe in his judgements of what he found to be primitive or provincial or wild.

His Anglican preferences were expressed: in Hawaii, Hiram Bingham, the American Protestant missionary "bumbled" along "in a most Methodistical" manner. Chilean Catholic priests were condemned as "blind" and "senseless" by him because they sought a "sign" from a young criminal on his deathbed.

But Dampier could be sympathetic and laudatory. If he did not approve of Hawaiian chiefs and South American Indians in general, he came to admire Boki and Venancio as individuals, almost as heroes. If, at times, he was amused by the customs of Chilean society, he was also delighted by the naturalness and friendliness of the members of that society. Tolling convent bells announcing the hour of evening prayer moved him to write an admiring and reverent account of Catholic devotions. Moreover, his own countrymen were not free from some ridicule. Dampier depicts the scramble for souvenirs from the ancient Hawaiian temple, Hale o Keawe, by some of the crew of the *Blonde* as a boisterous raid.

His particular Englishness increases the reader's enjoyment of the journal. The comparison of sweetened poi, that paste-like Hawaiian staple, with the sweet English dessert, fool, is an amusing surprise. His delight at seeing poke bonnets "made precisely after the English fashion" and worn by the native wives of the London Missionary

Society's native ministers at Mauke seems charmingly naïve. And his approval of their modesty in being "muffled closely" and wearing a length of *kapa* around their shoulders "in the same manner that an English lady would wear her shawl" indicates a gentle prudery typical of his times.

Perhaps the historian might regret the the lack of political analysis by Dampier. He attended a council of chiefs in Honolulu called to meet with Lord Byron to discuss "the state of the nation." He was in Chile when the new nation was attempting, not too successfully, to achieve political stability and he met many of the important leaders of the time. Yet political discussion in either area occupied his interest hardly at all. The battle he witnessed at Callao and the news of a war in Hawaii were fully recorded. But apparently he was indifferent to the complexities and subtleties of politics.

Perhaps this preference for nature and society in their visible manifestations gives the Dampier journal its special charm. To see the eastern Pacific with his youthful enthusiasm and his artist's sensitivity is to see the area in a most pleasurable form.

The journal published here was made available to the University of Hawaii Press by Lieutenant Commander Denis Dampier, Royal Navy (retired), of West Clandon, Surrey, England, who also supplied the biographical material. The journal had been presented to the artist's daughter, Matilda Elizabeth, and passed next to her nephew, Admiral Cecil F. Dampier, Royal Navy, grandson of Robert, and father of Denis. The present publication includes reproductions of thirty sketches which are part of the journal and of four portraits and two seascapes which are in collections in Hawaii. The copies of the portraits of Nahi'ena'ena and Kauikeaouli were made available through the courtesy of the Honolulu Academy of Arts. The Office of the Governor of the State of Hawaii granted permission for the inclusion of the copies of the portraits of the young chief and chiefess and the views of the *Blonde* at sea. The map on page vi detailing the track of H.M.S. *Blonde* was taken from the *Voyage of H.M.S. Blonde to the Sandwich Islands in the Years 1824–1825*.

Biographical Note

Robert Dampier was born in 1800 at Colford St. Peter's in Wiltshire, one of thirteen surviving children of the Reverend John Dampier. His forebears probably came from Flanders in the fifteenth century and settled in Lincolnshire in pursuit of some occupation in connection with the wool trade. They became prosperous merchants, property owners, and public officials in Lincolnshire. His grandfather, John, served as mayor of Wareham on four occasions between 1774 and 1795. His father took holy orders after leaving Oxford and began an association with the Church of England that remains a tradition to the present day.

The most well-known Dampier, William (1652–1715), buccaneer, captain in the British Navy, and circumnavigator, may have been of the same family stock as the diarist, but the relationship seems to be remote. William was a frequent visitor at the Galápagos Islands in the late seventeenth century. At that time Pacific buccaneers used the islands as a base for their raids against Spanish treasure ships. It is at least an interesting coincidence that two Dampiers were visitors to that strange and rarely visited region.

Robert left England in 1818 to become a clerk in the establishment of his brother-in-law, William May, a wealthy merchant in Rio de Janeiro. It was there, six years later, that the artist met Lord Byron. How he became acquainted with Byron can only be surmised. There is evidence that Byron knew of him and his family through acquaintances in the Navy. Perhaps, also, the artist's proficiency was well known in Rio. What is apparent is that the young man was given a preferred position on board the *Blonde*.

Upon his return to England, Dampier attended Cambridge University, first at Christ's College then at Corpus Christi College. By 1836 he had acquired a law degree and had also taken holy orders. Although he had charge of a country parish early in his career and again during the last years of his life, he spent most of his time traveling in Europe, or residing at his homes in Le Havre, France, or Guernsey, in the Channel Islands. In the words of his great-grandson, Denis, "One gets the impression . . . of a . . . man who lived in the spacious days when it was possible for a clergyman of private means to travel extensively and to devote much of his time to his leisure pursuits.

Not much is known of his life abroad but there seems to be a good deal of evidence that he spent as much of his time in painting as he did in preaching."

In 1828 Robert married Sophia, daughter of Colonel Elliott Roberts. There were four children: Frederick, who became chief magistrate of Georgetown, Demerara, British Guyana; Augustus, who took holy orders; Juliana, who married Sir William Robinson, governor of, at various times, the Bahamas, Barbados, Trinidad, and Hong Kong; and Matilda Elizabeth, who remained single. Dampier's first wife died in 1864, and he married again in 1872. A daughter, Frederika, was the only child of this marriage, and she remained single. The voyager-diarist-artist-clergyman died in 1874.

Published Accounts of the *Blonde*'s Voyage

There are at present three published accounts relating to the voyage of the *Blonde*. The earliest is the *Voyage of H.M.S. Blonde to the Sandwich Islands in the Years 1824–1825*, published in London in 1826. The work is a compilation of information gathered from diaries of various members of the expedition, in particular that of the Reverend Richard Bloxam, chaplain on board. Several of Dampier's sketches are included. Mrs. Maria Graham edited the book, and soon after its publication it was criticized in London as containing "flagrant inaccuracies." The fact that the work is a compilation limits its usefulness.

In 1922 those parts of the diary of James Macrae, botanist, specifically relating to the Hawaiian Islands were published in Honolulu. Macrae sailed on the *Blonde* at the request of the Horticultural Society of London, now the Royal Horticultural Society, with a collection of plants to be distributed in Hawaii. He had also been directed to collect plant specimens for the Society. Some incidents described by Macrae are found in the Dampier journal.

In 1925 the portions of Andrew Bloxam's diary relating to the Hawaiian Islands were printed in full by the Bernice P. Bishop Museum, and excerpts from the rest of the diary, interspersed with editorial comment, preceded and followed the quoted portion. Andrew, brother of the chaplain, Richard, was the naturalist on the *Blonde*. His short description of the visit to the temple at Honaunau contrasts sharply with Dampier's.

The present journal is the only one so far published that describes the entire voyage from the point of view of a single participant.

Note on the Spelling

American Protestant missionaries who arrived in Hawaii in 1820 began to put the Hawaiian language into a written form, and by January of 1822 an alphabet had been standardized. Material was being printed in the language and the final alphabet was produced in 1826.

Westerners had had difficulty in writing down the Hawaiian words they heard. For example, they often mistook the case sign attached to a proper name as part of the name. *Atooi* is a compound of two words, *a Tauai* which mean "and Tauai," the island of Tauai, or Kauai. Similarly, the *o* of *Owhyhee* is the sign of the nominative case of Whyhee, or Hawaii.

Vowel distinctions and variations of pronunciation also presented problems. The Reverend William Ellis, an expert in the Tahitian and Hawaiian languages, pointed out that there were no counterparts in English for certain Hawaiian vowel sounds, and some letters were interchangeable. Thus *Tauai* became *Kauai* in some regions; *Karaimoku* became *Kalaimoku*.

Dampier's spelling exemplifies a transitional stage. He arrived in Hawaii in 1825, after some Hawaiian had been printed but before the alphabet was settled upon. Hence his spelling shows only moderate variations. The form has been kept as it appeared in the diary, and variations are noted in the text.

The English usage of the early nineteenth century as reflected in Dampier's spelling and punctuation has been retained. Obvious misspellings have for the most part been corrected, however, the idiosyncrasies of Dampier's spelling have been kept. His practice of underlining words, not related to the modern practice of underlining for emphasis, has not been followed.

TO THE SANDWICH ISLANDS ON H.M.S. *BLONDE*

1
From Rio de Janeiro to Callao

On the 18th of December 1824 I left Rio de Janeiro, and embarked on board H.M. Frigate *Blonde*, commanded by the Right Honble Lord Byron, the principal object of whose voyage was to convey back to their kindred dust, the remains of the King and Queen of the Sandwich islands. The suite of the ill fated pair were also thus provided with an immediate opportunity of returning to their native country.

Having resided at Rio for the last six years, I should have been extremely unwilling to have gone back to England, without visiting the various countries of South America beyond Cape Horn, I therefore most joyfully embraced Lord Byron's kind proposal of allowing me to become a passenger with him.

It being difficult to procure stock at Rio, at the moment of our departure, we in consequence determined to touch at St. Catharine's [Brazil], where we hoped to collect a sufficient quantity, to supply our wants, until our arrival at Valparaiso [Chile].

On the 24th instant after a delighfully smooth passage we made the land in the vicinity of St. Catharine's, and finally, about eight o'clock in the evening anchored at the mouth of the harbour.

According to the very favorable accounts which have been given of this island, by Kotesbue [Kotzebue], and other quondam visitants, I expected to be much delighted with the beauty of the place: it did not however at all strike me, as equal in any degree, to the majestic views I had been so long in the habit of contemplating at Rio.

On the 25th (Xmas day,) we removed farther into the Bay, but owing to the very fresh breezes, to which it appears this harbour is peculiarly subject, we were unable to go on shore until the following day, when a Party of us landed at a small village on the main land, for the purpose of collecting our stock, which was not quite so abundant, or so easily procured as we had anticipated.

During the time we remained here, I accompanied Lord Byron to the town of St. Catharine's, from which our ship lay about nine miles. Having landed, we straightway bent our steps to the residence of the Governor, in order to make him a complimentary visit. His appearance certainly neither bespoke the dignity or state attached to the first man on the island. He was a most slovenly looking personage, possessing a long bilious mahogany visage, upon which were most decidedly marked the traces of discontent and ill-humour.

R.D. delt. 1826.

He however succeeded in relaxing the vinegar expression of his countenance into something meant for a smile of welcome, and after sundry compliments requested the favor of our company to dinner. Our alertness in accepting the offer, rather I think discomposed the old gentleman, as he quickly apologized for the wretched fare we should experience at his table. We had made up our minds however to put to the test the culinary qualifications of his "chef de cuisine," and until the great and important hour of dinner arrived, we sauntered about to see the town, which is prettily situated, and has a commodious harbour for vessels of small tonnage.

Having gratified our Curiosity, and purchased all the stock we could lay our hands upon, we again returned to our friend the President [Governor?] whose dinner upon the whole was not so bad—and the company of his lively little wife, amply made amends for all culinary deficiences. After dinner we bade adieu to our hospitable entertainers, and returned on board with our purchases of Pigs and Poultry.

We remained at anchor from the 25th to the first of January, during which time I took frequent strolls for the purpose of observing the face of the country, and also to acquire materials for a few sketches.

Our rigging being completely set in order for encountering the boisterous weather in rounding Cape Horn, we again made sail on New-Years day!

In a prosperous voyage of thirty-four days duration, very few events can possibly occur worthy of narration, at least by me, who do not presume to enter upon nautical details. I therefore content myself with remarking that our voyage proved excessively agreeable; being blest with smooth water, and fine weather during the whole passage, with the exception of a few boisterous hours when in the latitude of the river Plate [de la Plata]: this was the first time I experienced those delightful sensations accompanying a Noviciate on the seas in a gale of wind, and for some few hours I wondered at my having quitted so agreeable a place as Rio, for my present qualmish and stomach-rending situation.

With the foul winds—however, shortly vanished all these disagreeable and unpleasant symptoms, from which, by the subsequent very favorable weather, I was entirely relieved.

IO DE JANEIRO, BRAZIL
Majestic views"

On the 14th, we were in sight of the bleak icy looking mountains of Staten land, off which, we were becalmed for two days. Favoring breezes however, soon enabled us to round the dreaded Cape, and on the 4th of February, to my great delight we made the land not many miles distant from the harbour of Valparaiso. I had supposed I should have suffered greatly from the cold in rounding Cape Horn, the thermometer was never, during the most severe weather, lower than 39 degrees.

Having coasted along a most arid and unprofitable country, the harbour of Valparaiso suddenly opened upon us.

Notwithstanding I had been prepared for a barren looking and uncultivated spot, yet the wretched appearance of the town altogether surprised me exceedingly. Immediately beneath a high range of hills, whose unprofitable sides are thinly covered with brown underwood, and prickly pear, is situated the most fashionable part of the delightful town of Valparaiso, which consists of one long street running parallel with the sea shore, being removed a few yards only, from a heavy sandy beach. These hills are intersected by various ravines or vallies where, and on the sides of the hills, are built the huts of the poorer class of inhabitants, the houses being composed of mud, and exhibiting altogether a miserable picture of poverty and wretchedness.

The street in the town leads to a sandy plain called the Almendral, and extends to the distance of about three miles along the shore.

This is called the country, and in consequence, most of the merchants and richer class of inhabitants, reside in its neighbourhood. Here indeed you are a little relieved from the dull monotonous looking prospect constantly surrounding you, by the appearance of a few trees, which however are but sparingly distributed: these are mostly Olive, Apple, Pear, and other fruit trees.

Altho Nature has bestowed her blessings, thus niggardly upon this vale of Eden, conceiving I suppose, the possession of so delightful an appellation quite sufficient, still a stranger becomes quickly reconciled to these natural deprivations, owing to the great kindness and hospitality of the inhabitants, from whom I experienced every civility and attention. I allude to the English residents here, the Chileno's being mostly shop-keepers, or the lower class of tradespeople; so that, with the exception of two or three families, all my social intercourse was amongst my own countrymen.

In order to see as much as possible of the Country during our short stay here, I resolved upon visiting the Capital of Chili, which is situated about 90 miles from the Port.

Accordingly I made an arrangement for setting off in company with two officers of the Frigate, intending if possible, to perform our journey to the City in one day.

In order to accomplish this laborious feat, we had previously prepared three relays of horses to be in readiness at the different Post houses on the road.

We therefore (accompanied by our Peon, a sort of Guide whose office is also to assist us in saddling our horses, &c at the different Post houses on the road) all started early, in order to avoid as much as possible, the extreme heat of a vertical sun.

Our first stage was to a small village called Casa Blanca. Having ascended the high hills immediately surrounding Valparaiso, we arrived at the border of a vast plain, extending at least for twenty miles, where—

"Far as the eye could reach, no tree was seen,
Earth, clad in russet, scorn'd the lively green."

My companions being determined to try the celerity and mettle of their steeds, proceeded onward at a most active pace; little leisure was therefore allowed me for contemplating the scenery of the country through which, we were rapidly passing.

These vast plains, the first level ground we had seen since our arrival in Chili, (their perspective chequered with the distant figures of various horsemen arrayed in their country's picturesque and peculiar costume) notwithstanding their monotony, carried with them a grand and beautiful effect: the distant Andes in which they terminated, always assisting the sublimity of the scenery. On either side of the road or sandy path, vast flocks of large hawks and other birds of prey were assembled together: they scarcely deign'd to notice the presence of the passing traveller, and with immoveable gravity stood up, like so many centinels to their bleak, and unfrequented territories.

As our horses proceeded with unabated vigour, we quickly changed this wild scenery, and the country now wearing a more cultivated appearance, indicated our approach to Casa Blanca, where we soon arrived, having performed our first stage a distance of thirty six miles, in three hours.

This Village is composed of a few mud cottages, the most conspicuous habitation being our Post house, whose sign, quickly informed us, that good refreshment for man and horse, might easily be procured beneath its convenient roof.

I cannot here refrain from bestowing my tribute of praise, on the excellence of the Chilian horses: you are no sooner seated, than off you gallop, gallop, gallop, to the end of the chapter: not an idea of relaxation from these active exertions, enters into the head of either horse or rider, both being equally animated with the desire of getting on. Our Peon having caught with his "laço" a fresh relay of rough looking animals from a neighbouring enclosure, we again proceeded on our route, having previously taken the precaution of strengthening our insides with a good breakfast. Here I must pause to caution all future travellers who wish to profit by my experience, to supply the cravings of Nature very sparingly on the road; as the constant equestrian agitation causes great confusion and uneasiness, to a good meal.

We now proceeded with a fresh guide, fresh horses, and fresh spirits, at a most expeditious rate, thro a country which really began to wear a most beautiful aspect. On either side the road were extended thick woods, here and there interspersed with meadow and pasture land. A wonderfully level and straight road, took us to the foot of the Questa de Zapatá, a steep ascent sufficiently precipitous, to quell the speed of the most flyaway horse in existence. The Sun began to get intolerably hot, and the quantity of dust, hill, and heat, was quite overwhelming: we however soon succeeded in conveying ourselves to the top of this tremendous hill, and we were certainly amply compensated for our fatigue, in the contemplation of one of the most enchanting prospects I had ever beheld. I vainly endeavoured to delineate this heavenly scenery. But, owing to my own incapacity, and my Companions desire to keep moving I made but a poor sketch of

ST. CATHARINE, BRAZI
"A commodious harbour for vessels of small tonnage

it. Our horses and selves being now refreshed with a few minutes rest, away we again set off, as if possessed with the spirit of Tom Rapid himself, and in a few minutes, we were again on level ground, having descended the questa with a rapidity, greatly to the hazard of ourselves and horses. I here prevailed on my Companions to allow me a few minutes more to complete another sketch, after which our old spirit of galloping again continued.

The Sun had already exalted himself high in the heavens, and our spirits became in consequence as much depressed; both men and horses were quite overcome by his oppressive rays; we therefore very wisely determined to defer the completion of our journey until the afternoon, when we might take it coolly, and reach the City in the evening. We accordingly, during the heat, after taking a little refreshment, notwithstanding my former advice, quickly calmed our agitations by enjoying the benefit of a good siesta, at the next Post house, in which, were stretched out, raw hides, and mattresses, for the benefit and ease of all wayworn, joint shaken, bowel-jumbled, travellers, like ourselves.

At four in the afternoon we again proceeded to horse, the whole party feeling somewhat stiff, and not at all the better for past exertions. We however soon fell into our old habit of getting over the ground, more particularly owing to the comfortable intelligence which our Guide afforded us, who assured us, that the second mountain, the "Questa de Prao," over which we had to pass ere we arrived at the City, was much infested by a parcel of unceremonious fellows, who used no delicacy whatever in their manner of accosting benighted travellers, for, after robbing them, they filled up the measure of their attentions by deliberately murdering their victims.

We all simultaneously examined our Pistol's!!!—what a fine effect does this alarm give to a terrific description. Ere the Sun set, we had already arrived at the top of this heart quaking mountain, from the summit of which, looking towards the country we had then been traversing, one of the most grand prospects imaginable presented itself. The Sun was just setting, and the broad shadows from the Andes, and the misty vapours, flowing beneath their lofty summits, produced an effect most inexpressibly grand. I here again betook myself to my pencil, and having quickly delineated an hasty outline, we again pushed forward. This was the last mountain we had to cross, and the view on the other side which was suddenly presented to us, afforded an equally beautiful picture. We were now in sight of a very lofty chain of Mountains, their heights veiled in eternal snow, at whose base, the town of SantIago stretched itself, being scarcely discernible through the evening mists, which were gradually concealing the distant landscape: luckily for my reader's patience, Night suddenly closed in, veiling all objects in obscurity, he is therefore spared a further description on the subject.

At the foot of the mountain we found fresh horses provided for us, by a parcel of ill looking fellows, residing in two or three huts on the roadside. The villainous, and cunning features, of some of these men, called to our recollections, the unpleasant stories our Guide had recently been relating. Our former restless complaint therefore of pushing forward, again assailed us.

Immediately on our arrival at SantIago the Peon directed me to the residence of an English Merchant, to whom I had previously procured a letter of recommendation. He received me very civilly, and after lamenting his inability to lodge me, directed me to an English inn, the only one in the place: he expressed his hope of constantly seeing me at his table during my stay.

The accommodations of the inn were wretched in the extreme. Here then, I and my companions took up our quarters, and on the succeeding morning, sallied forth for the purpose of reconnoitring the town. A person who wishes to enjoy himself, must in the summer months, rise extremely early at SantIago. The mornings and evenings are the only periods of the day you can at all look about you; as the heat is intolerably oppressive.

Ere the Sun has attained any height, the temperature of the air is exceedingly cool and agreeable: the evenings also are rather cold than otherwise. This, so unusual in a warm climate, I suppose is accounted for, by the town's vicinity to the neighbouring Andes, whose majestic heights, crowned with a diadem of eternal snow, always assure to the town, a cool refreshing breeze, when not encountered by the strength and fierceness of a summer's sun. During the

MONTEVIDEO, URUGUAY
"In the latitude of the river Plate"

middle of the day until the afternoon, the inhabitants mostly confine themselves to the houses, and not a soul is seen traversing the solitary streets, with the exception, as is proverbially said, of a few dogs, and as many Englishmen.

Altho SantIago is removed at so short a distance from the Port of Valparaiso, yet the thermometer at the former place, must at least be eight or ten degrees higher. I certainly found it less suffocating and unpleasant than the heat of Rio: still, the Apathy, and want of activity in the inhabitants, surprised me, the case being widely different at Rio, where notwithstanding the great and more pernicious heat, the streets continue thronged, and business is carried on with unabated activity throughout the day.

I saw much to amuse and gratify me during my very limited stay at SantIago, and regretted very much, that the obligation of returning to the Port on the fourth day after our arrival, would not afford me sufficient time to become acquainted with Chileno manners, and Chileno society. The town in point of cleanliness infinitely surpasses the Capital of Brazil, and possesses a delightful advantage in being constantly irrigated by the waters of the Maypocho [Mapocho].

It stands on an extensive plain, and occupies a considerable portion of ground, owing to the peculiar construction of the houses, which, from the frequency of earthquakes are all built on a ground floor.

The streets cross each other at right angles, and are well paved, possessing an advantage so necessary in a warm climate, of having a stream of water constantly flowing in a narrow channel through the Centre of each of them.

A stranger, accustomed to the liveliness of a European town, is particularly struck with the gloomy appearance of the streets, as the houses, instead of presenting rows of windows, are completely shut out from your view by a wall, which forms a part of a square, into which, the various windows of the house have their aspect. In the midst of this Court, are planted a variety of fruit trees, which contribute greatly to give an air of Coolness to the rooms thus situated. The inhabitants also secure to themselves an immediate escape into an open space, in case of the sudden visitation of an earthquake.

To each of these Courts, is an immense gateway, from the staff on the top of which, depends on all holidays and fête days, the National flag, a custom I believe prevailing, thro all towns on this side of South America.

In the very Centre of the City, a curious rock entirely composed of grey granite, abruptly rises; it completely commands the whole town, and on its heights is erected, a small, and insignificant fortress. The environs of the town are picturesque and beautiful. On all sides, the bright verdure of trees of every shade of green, from the shadowy fig tree, to the brilliant poplar, especially when contrasted by the Andes, rising in awful solemnity in the background, form a grand and interesting picture; added to which, is the costume of the Peasantry of the Country, the ample folds, and varied tints of whose Poncho's, contribute greatly to the beauty and novelty of the scene.

While remaining here I constantly visited the Baths, which may certainly be accounted one of the greatest luxuries which this town possesses. They were quite close to our inn, and are I think extremely well regulated and much resorted to. Ices also, another luxury in so warm a climate are easily procured. Fruits of every description seemed to thrive in great abundance, indeed, the Gardens and Orchards immediately surrounding the town, appeared most prolific.

Notwithstanding the heat of the weather, I took frequent rides into the country round about the City, and from a neighbouring Mountain was enabled to take a pretty accurate outline, comprehending a most extensive view of the Andes, as well as the town beneath my feet.

I also paid a visit to the "Salta de Agua" about 5 miles distance; it has little else than a beautiful ride to recommend it to a strangers notice.

You leave the town at one quarter, & after an hours ride, arrive at the foot of a very steep hill, from whence descends this very insignificant waterfall.

On returning, you enter the town by a different route, but the inclination is so very gradual, that you hardly perceive that any can exist, notwithstanding the steep Mountain you had previously been ascending.

There are two very pretty public walks here, to which, the Beau

Monde daily resort in the afternoon, after the heat of the day has somewhat subsided. I here had an opportunity of contemplating all that was elegant and fashionable at SantIago.

The men I pass over in silence, their appearance indicating a very inferior class of beings—Not so the women. Here indeed, Fame had not erred in allotting so large a portion of beauty to the fair sex at SantIago. I saw very many pretty faces, and the graceful elegance, and native ease, so perceptible in a Chileno beauty, completely rivetted my attention to objects so peculiarly interesting.

They have generally beautiful black eyes, whose soft lustre is very much heightened by their remarkably clear, and rosy complexions: added to this, they possess good figures and walk gracefully.

I observed with regret, that Custom has induced the ladies to desert almost entirely the elegant Spanish mantilla, whose place is now almost universally supplied by dresses made in the height of English and French fashions.

I now returned musing to my inn, fully assuring myself, that I might sojourn at SantIago very agreeably for a month or six weeks.

An English Lady assured me that the education of these pretty creatures was so much neglected, that they barely possessed sufficient ingenuity to write their own names, many not being advanced even thus far in their literary attainments. Of course this must have been a scandal of her own invention.

Our Party now determined to return to the Port of Valparaiso, as we had received intelligence, that the *Blonde* would be ready for sea in a few days.

As we had already experienced what an intolerable companion a hot burning sun had been to us during our journey to the City, we now determined to give him as little of our company as possible, we therefore left the city at two o'clock in the morning, and by rising thus early, found ourselves at our journey's end, at about 3 o'clock in the afternoon.

Nothing remarkable occurred on the road. Our Guide did not furnish us with such good horses on our return jaunt, which as may naturally be supposed, caused some little delay and inconvenience. Two of these poor animals thought it prudent to desist entirely from all further exertions, notwithstanding we used the most strenuous of all arguments, to prove our diversity of opinion.

Upon our arrival we found out, that the Small Pox had spread itself on board our ship. This unseasonable visitation caused Lord Byron the utmost anxiety and distress, as it would be utterly impossible to proceed in this state to the Sandwich islands, incurring the hazard of depopulating and exterminating the whole race of Sandwichers.

It was therefore determined, after having deposited all that were infected with the disorder in the hospital at Valparaiso, to give all hands the benefit of a short cruize of a week or ten days, we should then allow sufficient time to elapse, in order to ascertain, if the Disorder had departed with those infected.

I forgot to mention, that Kapihe, one of the Sandwich Chiefs, bearing the rank of Admiral, died a few days after our arrival at Valparaiso.

His decease was caused by an influx of blood to the head, brought on principally, by his devout, and frequent libations, in honour of the rosy God.

On the 19th we left Valparaiso, purposing to make the island of Juan Fernandez. A small cutter which Lord Byron had engaged to accompany him to the Sandwich isles, also sailed with us.

The wind proved quite unfavorable to our intention of visiting this island, and moreover, by its boisterous and troublesome conduct, completely convinced us, that the Pacific Sea, notwithstanding its placid name, could boil and foam like other seas. Indeed our voyage proved disagreeable in the extreme. With the expectation of fine weather, all the skuttles in the Gunroom were left open, consequently, the luckless inhabitants of the different Cabins to which they afforded light, were deluged with salt water.

As there were no hopes of our reaching Juan Fernandez, after beating about, for four or five days, we again, to our great delight, bore up for Valparaiso, where we anchored on the 24th of February.

During the whole of this time no new case of small pox had appeared on board, we therefore began to comfort ourselves with the assurance, that so relentless a companion had entirely forsaken us.

We remained here for the space of ten days—these my various

ALPARAÍSO, CHILE
Beneath a high range of hills"

delt 1826

friends endeavoured to make as agreeable as possible, one by the loan of a horse,—another—a bed—and all, amply providing good eating and drinking, little attentions greatly appreciated by a sojourner in a strange land.

Thus, having a good horse always at my command, I made myself more acquainted with the neighbouring country around Valparaiso.

On all sides the same barren and dreary appearance constantly prevails, the quebradas or ravines however, which are interspersed about these hills, form exceptions: these, from generally enjoying the moistening influence of a small rivulet trickling thro' their centre, afford a few patches of green, indeed, some of them are highly cultivated, and produce, in a very small space, a great quantity of fruit and vegetables.

With these articles, the Market of Valparaiso is plentifully supplied, tho the greater part is conveyed from villages at some distance from the town.

It is almost surprising to state, that notwithstanding Dame Nature has been thus sparing in affording such slight covering for the nakedness of the land, yet the juvenile part of the inhabitants here is strangely addicted to the pleasure, if so it may be called of "PicNic" parties.

I was invited to attend several of these excursions. A Party having been formed, each Gentleman is obliged to furnish a pair of holsters, whose destructive tenants are turned out, to give place to others, which, though not quite so dangerous to corporeal, yet often prove fatal to mental faculties. From this I hope it is understood, that each Male Visitant is armed with a couple of Bottles of Wine, by way of rendering him a fitter subject for taking care of the female part of the Community, who undertake to provide the eatables.

The Search then commences under a burning Sun, for some sheltering tree or running stream, where the Parties may collect to eat, drink, and be Merry!

After much difficulty this grand object is accomplished, and the important occupation of filling our stomachs immediately follows. These are called holster parties. I enjoyed myself very much during several of these excursions, for Merry Companions, and good cheer amply compensated, for the absence of purling streams, shady trees, and such other rural delights, as "PicNic"ers are in the habit of enjoying.

As his Lordship felt almost confident the Small Pox had left the ship, no new cases nor symptoms having appeared since our former cruize, he determined to sail immediately. We therefore left the Port of Valparaiso on the 5th of March with the intention of touching at Chorillos. Carrying with us a fair wind, on the eighth day we anchored at this place: it is a fine, and commodious bay, and situated about four or five leagues from Callao and within nine miles of the city of Lima, whose towers and cupolas were distinctly visible from our deck as we entered the harbour.

We here found the *Cambridge* (80 Gun ship) together with several Chilian and Peruvian men of war, as also a great variety of Merchant ships, anxiously awaiting the fall of Callao, which at the moment was closely besieged by the army of Bolivar.

If the view of the coast of Chili strikes a stranger as barren and unfruitful, how much more must he be surprised when contemplating the glaring and sandy coast of Peru. Scarcely any vegetation seems to flourish, except in the immediate vicinity of Lima. This city, I regret much to say, I was unable to visit, as our intention was that of sailing on the following morning. In the afternoon I went on shore at Chorillos. If this place looked uninviting from the ship, a nearer examination caused no alteration in my opinion of its attractions. The village has a most singular appearance, being situated on the verge of a plain, abruptly rising from the sea, to the height of about 100 feet.

I succeeded in drawing a panorama, which pretty accurately points out the local peculiarities of the country. Upon landing, which I effected upon a ledge of rocks, only I should think accessible in fine weather, I was obliged to climb a steep ascent, the walk rendered more tedious and unpleasant, from the great quantity of loose gravel and sand, constantly sliding from beneath your feet. Arrived at the top, one of the most wretched looking villages imaginable presented itself to my speculations. Owing to the earthquakes, so often prevailing, most of the houses are roofed with reed, the walls also are composed of the same, and are plaistered over with mud.

It must be remembered, that the arid and burnt up soil of Peru,

◁ SANTIAGO, CHILE
"In sight of a very lofty chain of mountains"

SANTIAGO, CHILE ▷
"In the very Centre of the City . . . a small, and insignificant fortress"

is never refreshed with a single drop of rain throughout the year, solidity of material in building is therefore not required by a Peruvian artificer.

The inhabitants bear a great Analogy to the appearance of the huts they reside in. They are a wretched looking race, and the lank black hair, flat faces, and small eyes of the Peasantry, immediately announce their strong affinity to the primitive Indians of the Country. Here, as well as in Chili, such clouds of dust are continually colled [rolled?] along, that eyes, nose, and mouth, are constantly assailed; indeed, to venture upon an observation, or to regard objects too intensely, almost endangers a person's eyesight if perchance he escapes suffocation. The aerial inhabitants of this Neighbourhood are most extraordinary looking animals, consisting of vast flocks of immense black Vultures, about the size of a Turkey. Almost every roof in the village is honoured with two or three of these impish guests, even the Church, sacred in all other respects, is quite defiled with crowds of them. They appear like so many "Harpies" ready to pounce upon any tit-piece of carrion that may present itself.

I believe they are of the Anthropophagi [man-eating] species, as some little time since, an engagement took place between a Party of Spanish and Peruvian troops, in consequence of which, about two hundred were left dead on the field of action, which was a short distance from Chorillos. Their remains were immediately devoured by these birds, such useful members of society do they thus evince themselves. There is a heavy penalty attached to the offence of destroying them. As I had now gratified my curiosity, I returned on board, and was much delighted at hearing, that on the succeeding morning, we were to accompany the *Cambridge* to Callao, to see how the Belligerent powers were amusing themselves.

We accordingly weighed on the morrow, and towards the evening, in company with the *Cambridge* stood out from the land. On the succeeding day we anchored in Callao Roads, about half a mile distant from the Fort, which, together with the town, are situated immediately upon the seashore.

It appears to be a fortification of wonderful strength, and will I have no doubt cause the Limanians an infinity of trouble, and hard fighting, ere they can prevail upon its present sturdy possessor Rodil, to listen to terms of Capitulation.

Being invited this day to dinner with Capt. Maling, on board the *Cambridge*, I proceeded thither immediately upon his anchoring.

From her Poop I had an opportunity of witnessing a little skirmishing between Rodil's and Bolivar's foraging parties: it was a nervous sight to observe how dexterously the men composing the latter party, evaded the hostile shot continually levelled at them from the batteries. We could distinctly observe each shot as it alighted on the ground.

Thus we were amused until dinner time, after which important and active attack, on our part, a new scene by way of des[s]ert presented itself to us, all which, no doubt had been got up between Rodil and his Adversary, solely for our amusement. I trust I am not giving them credit for any overstrained act of Politeness and Attention towards us.

The Fort of Callao had been constantly blockaded by two Peruvian men of war. To these were attached two Gun boats, which no doubt, to give us an idea how their GUNS would carry, came in at the distance of about a mile from the shore, and with a couple of 32 Pounders, caused the mud and mortar of the Callao houses, to fly about in all directions. These were answered by the large Guns on the top of the Fort.

It was certainly startling for one of peaceable habits like myself, to see the Gun Boats evidently in so much danger. Every shot from the Forts, which passed very near us, threw an angry splash almost into the Boats. However, "a miss is as good as a mile," and the little boats, notwithstanding their powerful adversaries, still maintained their system of demolition.

At length, after a sudden bustle on shore, six small Spanish Gun boats suddenly pushed off from the Beach. The gallant Patriots, had now a most unequal combat to sustain, after having removed themselves from the shore batteries, they now devolved their particular attention upon the Spanish gun boats.

A brisk firing of half an hours duration was kept up by the contending parties, and I am glad to add, that the pleasure and interest we all took in a sight so novel, was not of a sanguinary nature, as, altho' many shot fell within a few feet of the Boats on either side, none had

◁ CHORILLOS, PERU
"A fine, and commodious bay"

CALLAO, PER
"The fort . . . situated immediately upon the seashore

R. D. delt 1826.

the desired effect, and very shortly the Peruvians finding that in a given time, six Gunboats would throw shot much more plentifully than two, withdrew, having impressed us with great admiration at their gallant behaviour.

The day after the effusion of this contending spirit, an Aid-de-Camp of Rodil's came on board the *Cambridge* with an excuse from his Master for not seeing Capt. Maling and Lord Byron. They had previously sent, intimating their wish to pay him a visit.

Villacão, the Aid de Camp, spoke in high terms of the resources still possessed by the Garrison to protract the siege—they have about 2,000 men in the Forts, which certainly are impregnable: they can only starve them out.

Bolivar is now directing his attention to cut off their supplies of water.

Rodil, altho' an excellent officer, sullies his reputation by repeated acts of the most detestable cruelty: He conceives the utmost severity of discipline, the only mode of keeping his small force in fighting order. This day, neither Party feeling inclined to renew the contest, we again weighed anchor and in the Course of the afternoon tried our rate of sailing with the *Cambridge*. In the evening of the 4th [17th] Lord Byron wished his friends a long Farewell, and we then steered directly for the Galápagos, a small group of islands about 1,110 miles to the Northward of Callao.

2 The Galápagos Islands

Having a favorable wind, on the seventh day after our departure from Callao, we made Charle's Island [Santa Maria] Gallapagos; as we did not intend anchoring, until our arrival at Bank's cove [Bahía de Banks], a snug and secure anchorage in Albermarle Island [Albemarle or Isabela]. We coasted along in the hopes of coming to our place of destination, on the succeeding day.

Among these islands, we had to encounter battling winds, and contrary currents, it was not therefore until the evening of the 27th March, that we arrived in Bank's Cove.

Our object in visiting these islands, was that of procuring Wood, Water, Terepin and Turtle—the sequel will show how much our expectations were disappointed.

The heat was felt by us most oppressively, and the thermometer seldom declined below 84 or 85. It may be imagined therefore, that all hands were in a terrible stew.

The islands as we coasted along them, presented to our view a most extraordinary appearance: dark frowning rocks extended themselves to the waters edge. A successive chain of Volcanic craters added to the novelty of the scene. Indeed, almost all the islands are entirely composed of volcanic substance.

Narboro island [Narborough, Fernandina], on which there is an immense Volcano continually blazing forth, is one entire mass of purple lava, only relieved here and there, by small portions of very bright green brushwood.

On Sunday evening about 8 ⁰Clock, we entered this snug little harbour called Bank's Cove. As the water was extremely deep, we anchored within two hundred yards of the shore. Our remote and unknown situation, is certainly worthy of particular description. As we silently proceeded, gliding almost imperceptibly into the Cove, the strange inhabitants of a place so seldom visited by the Lords of the Creation, appeared rather uneasy at our approach, and continually gave utterance to the most unearthly sounds, expressive of their disapprobation at our unreasonable intrusion into their exclusive territories. A continual concert of voices was kept up throughout the night, and I longed for morning to make me acquainted with such strange Performers.

On Monday at daybreak, I accompanied our first Lieutenant to survey the watering place, which we were given to understand by the Master of the Cutter, was about a quarter of a mile from the Cove. It being calm, we rowed along within a boat's length of a precipitate ledge of rocks, forming a part of the Cove. It was at this time that we became personally acquainted with our strange serenaders of the preceding evening, and as the morning began to dawn, various uncouth animated objects presented themselves to our view.

Whole regiments of Boobies and Penguins, sat with becoming gravity on the shelving rocks; whilst every projecting point was graced with the presence of a dowdy Pelican, eagerly looking out for his accustomed meal, and distending his vast pouch, in anticipation of an early breakfast: added to these, were a vast variety of all sorts of sea birds, pluming their feathers, and by their billing, whistling and clapping their wings, preparing no doubt for their mornings excursions. Dark lava rocks were scattered immediately below, forming in some places very deep caverns, sacred to the Sea Lion, Seals, and other Monsters of the deep, which tho not yet visible, inform'd us of their presence by sundry groans, hisses, and other diabolical sounds. The surface of these rocks was compleatly covered with large black Sea Guana's or lizards. These, of all the animals I ever saw, strike me as most disgusting: indeed, if ever Satan felt inclined to become a tenant of some hideous and appropriate form upon earth, I certainly would recommend one of these devilish looking Monsters to his consideration. They herded together in such vast mobs, that really the rocks upon which they lay listlessly stretched out, were quite concealed from our view. One of our men with the natural thoughtlessness of sailors, grasped a boathook and with one mighty blow, laid prostrate about a dozen. The Survivors, to our great astonishment, were not at all dismayed at this violent execution, but with stoical indifference, awaited their share of such a rude salutation.

Another Man with an Oar, attacked an advanced division of Penguins, which were all swept down as suddenly as a Congreve Rocket would perform a similar execution, on a file of soldiers.

Owing to a heavy surf, we with difficulty landed, and proceeded to reconnoitre the watering place. Alas! here we were doomed to be sadly disappointed. The Master of the Cutter, who was our Guide and informant, (he having been here frequently before) conducted us to the spot where we were to find a great abundance of this precious fluid. Scarcely a drop was to be found, the place he pointed out not containing above a bucket full: indeed, I saw no appearance indicating, that water ever could have existed there, at least, in any quantity. We were entirely surrounded by rocks, and as Moses with his wand, was not of our party, we disconsolately had to return to the ship. We previously however took a view of the surrounding country.

Lava in all shapes and forms, abundantly prevails here, from immense rocks, to crumbling black dust. No trees of any height were to be seen: here and there a few bright green shrubs, were sparingly distributed. As we advanced into the island, these flourished more abundantly. We saw no animals, with the exception of the land Guana, which is about two feet long, of a bright harvest colour, and not differing from others of the lizard species. He is certainly a much more wholesome looking fellow than any of his marine brethren. A very limited variety of land birds seems to frequent these islands. I only saw three or four of different species, and those, small, and in no way remarkable for brilliancy of plumage. There is a small Dove however, whose plumage is very lively and beautiful. So tame were these unsuspecting inhabitants, that it was almost possible to catch them with your hand: indeed, one bird actually alighted on the muzzle of my Companion's Gun, "they were so unacquainted with man."

We now returned to the ship, with the unpleasant intelligence of the fruitlessness of our search for water. It was therefore determined, as we had still a long voyage to undertake, to put the ship's company on an immediate allowance of water, and from that time, we received six pints per day. According to this computation, the water remaining was to last us for fifty days. After breakfast, I accompanied Lord Byron on a fishing party. We placed ourselves in a boat a few yards from the rocks, and having cast in our lines, very quickly hauled up a vast quantity of fish, some of which were most curious looking creatures. One species I remarked with dark blue body, and bright yellow head. Another that we hooked, began distending his body in

BAHÍA DE BANKS, ALBEMARLE ISLAND, GALÁPAG
"Within a boat's length of a precipitate ledge of rock

such a manner, that I suspected we should have a scene from the Arabian tales, and that our entangled victim, bursting into a cloud of smoke, would suddenly appear to our eyes, a formidable genius, or an enchanted Demon.

In a very short time we caught a sufficiency of fish, and in the course of the morning, went on shore, to a small spot of ground, on which were erected two huts, the temporary residences of some part of the crew of a whaler, which had recently left the island. We found a small boat, and some prepared seal skins in a hut, at the mouth of the Cove, with an inscription in chalk, intimating that the persons to whom they belonged, were gone out for a cruize, and intended returning in a short time. In these huts, the Sandwich people took up their abode during our stay here, Lord Byron, having appropriated one of the boats entirely to their service. They seemed to enjoy themselves exceedingly, for here, they in some measure resorted to their pristine habits: their cuisine was also served up to their peculiar goût, which was that of devouring fish raw, immediately it was taken from the water.

In the course of the afternoon, Lord Byron in company with myself and two of his officers, took a sail in his boat for the purpose of visiting a Neighbouring beach, which we were given to understand, was the favorite resort of a vast quantity of turtle.

We landed on a fine sandy beach, from which, about 20 yards, was a Salt water lake, communicating with the sea.

Here, clusters of mangrove trees flourished in great abundance, and tho' no turtle appeared, we could plainly trace the places where they had deposited their eggs. As we were proceeding in our search, on the margin of the lake, we suddenly disturbed a Sea Lion and as suddenly, a couple of balls were buried in his luckless hide.

Notwithstanding, after a few uncouth flounders, he escaped without further molestation, and having secreted himself in the mangrove trees, gave vent to his displeasure, by sundry groans and low moanings. Shortly after, we perceived a large Turtle swimming along in the midst of the lake, upon which, one of our Boat's crew, "accoutred as he was plung'd boldly in," and after a few struggles, succeeded in hauling him on shore, where, having safely deposited him on his back, we recommenced our search.

ALT WATER LAKE, ALBEMARLE ISLAND, GALÁPAGOS
We suddenly disturbed a sea lion"

As the evening was fast approaching, we were obliged to desist from extending our walk, and therefore returned on board. On our arrival, we were agreeably surprised to find, that a Boat, which had been dispatched to an island opposite the Cove, had returned laden with 40 fine turtle. This boat, had left the ship early in the morning for this purpose, and had there been room, could have supplied her with double that number.

It was now determined, that we should not remain more than another day. All the Boats were therefore immediately put in requisition, in order that a sufficient quantity of wood might be collected for the ship's immediate use,—and his Lordship, having formed a little PicNic with myself and several others, proceeded to reconnoitre the vicinity of the Cove, and should perchance a shady spot offer itself, in this region of rocks, and yawning Volcano's, we determined to ruralize, and make ourselves comfortable with a good meal, which he had prepared for our consuming abilities. We landed not very distant from the place we had visited the preceding evening. The Sun was exceedingly powerful and the heated sand over which we were obliged to trudge, soon put a stop to our pedestrian exertions. We therefore laid aside our idea of exploring the country, and the only remaining anxiety, was, that of finding a shady spot, where we might dine in comfort.

As Nature had not been beneficent enough to furnish this part of the island with else than groups of lava rocks, and mangrove trees, their roots immersed in water, we were finally obliged to erect a sort of Tent, under whose protection from the sun, we managed remarkably well. As the afternoon advanced, the Sun lost much of his power, I therefore took a walk, for the purpose of observing the wonders of the place. On all sides, immense Pelicans, and other curious sea birds, were gliding heedlessly past us, all evincing, the most perfect indifference at our presence. I cannot forbear remarking the conduct of a small bird, which I almost felt inclined to punish for his want of respect to my Person: as I was busily employed in severing a mangrove branch, from its Parent tree, this most forward of the Feathered tribe, alighted close to my hand, and with the most unprecedented insolence, amused himself in pecking at the parings, as they fell in quick succession from the tree. The Pelicans and Sea

Guanas seemed equally unconscious of our murderous intentions towards them, the Seal alone seems to possess the most instinctive apprehensions of our destructive inclinations, and when caught on shore, invariably (may I say) "takes to his heels" by rapidly jumping, thumping and whirling about like a blown bladder when set in motion on the ground, & contrives to get out of your way, very successfully. I witnessed a hard fought struggle between our Surveyor and one of these Sea Monsters.

This Gentleman suddenly intercepted a mighty Sea Lion's retreat to the watery element, to which as a place of safety, he was rapidly advancing in the graceful manner I before described. The combat was long. I cannot say bloody, the sanguinary scene took place after the action. The Surveyor, armed with a boat's stretcher, laid about him most manfully, his powerful adversary however, was invulnerable in every place, saving, not as the mighty Achilles, in the heel, but rather in the Nose.

After sundry inflictions most unremittingly applied, which caused the Surveyor's opponent to show his tusks, and grin most horribly, a well aim'd blow, full on the vulnerable point, fell'd the monster to the ground: then the triumphant victor, in imitation of the heroes of old who invariably despoiled the vanquished of their arms, in a moment with his knife ripped up the skin from the body, and returned, like a second Hercules, with the bloody spoils of the Nemean Lion, at his back.

I, in the mean time, more peaceably inclined, seated myself on the sand, and tho' not much tempted by the beauty of the prospect, contrived to make a couple of sketches of the barren, tho' singular looking prospect, which presented itself.

As we had now amused ourselves very pleasantly during the day, we prepared for our departure, and on returning on board, were surprised at the sight of a ship coming in, with the intention of anchoring, which she did, not many miles distant from the place we had left. We ascertained the next day, that she was an American whaler, bound for the Sandwich Islands, and had visited this place in order to procure wood.

We had now the benefit of a beautiful moon, whose still silvery light, reflected on the placid sheet of water around us, when contrasted by the fiery lurid glare, constantly emitted from the opposite islands, formed a fine subject for a picture, highly characteristic, and interesting.

On the morning of the 30th, we weighed anchor, and gently receded from the cove into the midchannel. In the mean time, Lord Byron, Mr. Malden, and myself, went on shore at the top of the Cove, for the purpose of viewing a curious Salt Water pond in its vicinity. By taking a wrong path, we were unable to find out the place. On our return, we were startled by the appearance of a Dog, which belonged to one of the officers, and had been reported to have left him raving mad, on the preceding day. Unwilling to partake of the poor animal's disorder, we armed ourselves with stones, and prepared to stand on the defensive. We soon ascertained however, that all fears were groundless, as the poor dog had recovered his senses, which were quickly impelling him, to find the shortest way to our boat. We therefore gave him a passage off. The poor beast was so thirsty, that we could scarcely prevent him from swallowing the salt water at the bottom of the Boat.

On the 1st of April, we passed close to the Redondo island [Rosa Redonda], a curious looking rock, having much the resemblance of a tea table, on a gigantic scale.

Lord Byron allowed some of our Sandwich friends to spend an hour in their favorite amusement of fishing: they caught vast quantities under the base of this rock.

The day following, we made Abingdon's island [Pinta], where we hoped to get a large supply of Terepin, which are considered much more palatable and better flavoured than Sea Turtle. How fallacious are all human expectations! We were for several hours within a few miles of this island, but owing to baffling winds, and a rapid current, setting strongly against us, we were unable to go on shore, and consequently, deferred our Terepin feast, until a more convenient season.

We had already been detained a week among these Robinson

ALBEMARLE ISLAND, GALÁPAGC

"Immense Pelicans, and other curious sea birds

Crusoe looking islands, disappointed in our expectation of procuring water, and Terepin, and equally dissatisfied with our unprofitable detention. We found ourselves clear of them on the 3rd, but for several days were attended by light winds, and heavy rains. However we finally got possession of a fair wind, and have hitherto averaged 130 knots per day, since we left the Galapagos.

This may certainly be termed a most prosperous Voyage. We are now within seventy miles of OWhyhee [Hawaii], and tomorrow will I trust usher in

—"the great the important day,

Big with the fate of"—Boki and his Suite.

Various are the Conjectures respecting the state of these islands. All these will most likely be cleared up upon the morrow. I therefore forbear offering any opinion.

3

Hawaii: Hilo to Honolulu

May 3rd 1825

Early on the morning of this eventful day, we were delighted with the appearance of land on our starboard bow. The particular place we were now making, was a harbour in the district of Hido [Hilo], OWhyee; very justly celebrated for its excellent water. As we neared the land, to which, having a strong breeze we were rapidly approaching, our Sandwich friends seem'd to evince some little anxiety, with regard to the reception they were to experience from their countrymen.

They certainly hailed their Native land with very different looks and manners, to those which would appear in us, upon making Spithead. Boki and his wife appear'd somewhat dejected. I sincerely hope, they have not begun to prize the comforts, and advantages, which their late trip to England has so abundantly afforded them, too dearly:—they may perhaps, have just learnt sufficient to make themselves dissatisfied with the comparative state of savage ignorance and barbarity to which, they must soon again relapse. The sequel of Madame Boki's conduct throughout the day, will I think prove the truth of my observation.

The harbour of Hido is mentioned by Vancouver, as possessing no convenient situation for anchoring: this however has been strongly denied by one of the Chiefs on board, a very intelligent man, (who has acquired sufficient knowledge of our language, to act in all cases, as interpreter) who presented to Lord Byron a day or two before our arrival, a small chart of his own delineation.

According to this, it appeared, that should the Chief be in the right, this place would do uncommonly well to refit in. We therefore proceeded close in, to a large commodious Bay. On all sides the Country was clothed with a great variety of trees, and patches of bright verdure, and what, to our eyes appeared most delightful, were several majestic waterfalls, immediately emptying themselves into the sea.

About this time, we perceived three canoes busily employed in fishing. As we speedily came up with them, they hauled in their lines, and being hailed by one of their Chiefs in their native tongue,—the foremost in which were three men, paddled towards the ship.—When they appeared alongside, Madame Boki, quite shocked at the barbarous appearance of her almost naked countrymen, retired to her cabin. This delicate Lady, a few months since, was just as much disencumbered of her cloathes as the savages before her. Her fame, as being the best swimmer, and one, who would go thro' a heavy surf, before any of her less daring Companions, is universally acknowledged.

Perhaps, this assumption of Modesty was put on to suit our English ideas, and her present civilized situation. We prevailed upon one of these men to come on board. He seemed however, by the time, he put his foot on the quarter deck, to have repented of the temerity which had led him thus far. I never beheld a poor fellow in such a trepidation: every point [joint?] shook with excess of fear and astonishment, at his novel situation. These apprehensions soon leaving him, he possessed sufficient information to acquaint Boki, that Karaimoku [Kalanimoku] upon whose life, almost depended the thread of his own existence, was lingering under a dangerous disorder. He further gave some indistinct accounts, respecting a war, which had lately been going forward at one of the neighbouring islands. This man, as also several others who came on board, seemed indifferently, and weakly formed. Boki told us, they were mountaineers, and that at Oahu, we should see a much finer race of men.

Shortly afterwards, while we were yet "laying to," uncertain how to proceed, a Prussian Sailor came on board. This fellow could talk the English language remarkably well, and officiously recommended himself, by assuring us, he could take the ship into good anchorage. He also gave us further information, respecting the state of the islands, and the late war.

It appears, that the Governor of the isle of Atooi [Kauai] lately died, and that his son, who had been brought up in America, on returning to his native land, determined upon the first occasion that offered itself, to resist the power of the established government of Karaimoku. Upon the death of his Father, he conceived the propitious moment had arrived, for commencing an insurrection. Hearing of his purpose by some secret channel, Karaimoku immediately appointed a Chief of his own blood, and dispatched him with a suitable train of followers, to take possession of the island, and exercise his rights as Governor. His landing was opposed by the disaffected son of the deceased Chief, who, having possession of the Fort, immediately levelled the Guns at the new Governor, which hostile salute quickly dispersed the whole suite.

The intelligence of these proceedings were instantly brought to Karaimoku, who forthwith collecting a large force from the other islands, sailed to Atooi, attacked, and discomfited the rebellious powers, and put an end to the warfare, by taking the disaffected Chief a prisoner. As our Prussian visitor was recounting the military exploits of Karaimoku, our attention was suddenly arrested by boisterous exclamations, proceeding from a canoe coming up with the ship. Upon its nearer approach, another Pilot of Welch extraction stepped on board, and assured us, that the Ship was fast approaching a bar which ran immediately across the harbour. All, in an instant, was bustle and trepidation. Relying upon the information of a person, we supposed acquainted with the place, we of course put the Ship about as quickly as possible, and having as we conceived, escaped from the impending danger, we dispatch'd boats in the direction where the bar lay; when it was ascertained, that altho' it did exist, yet its situation was at least two miles nearer the shore, than our Ship lay at the moment. Having had this sample of the knowledge of the pilots of this country, we shall know how to trust to their assertions on future occasions.

The Master of the Frigate, together with Mr. Malden the Surveyor, being dispatched in two different Boats, to ascertain the exact sounding, and what depth of water existed nearer the shore, the Ship lay to, about six miles from the land until their return. In the mean time, several canoes came paddling around us, in order that the Natives might gratify their curiosity, with the nearer view of a ship, the largest that had ever appeared on this coast.

Some of these Canoes were beautifully constructed, and capable of carrying six or eight men. They are long, and uncommonly narrow, barely allowing sufficient room for the body of a man to introduce itself between the sides. The lower part of the Canoe is composed of a beautiful black wood, the extremities, which curve upwards something like the prow of an ancient Galley, are entirely carved out of a fine yellow wood, and altogether finished with a neatness & attention

HILO BAY, HAWA

"A harbour . . . celebrated for its excellent water

to the rules of architecture, truly surprising. Each canoe has two large poles about half its length, their ends sloping downwards proceeding from the gunnel, in a horizontal direction; to these, is firmly lashed another pole, of the same dimensions, its extremities curved upwards, which is lashed, in a parallel direction with the canoe like the fishing boats of Ceylon. This piece of simple machinery, prevents the canoe from upsetting, which disaster, considering how narrow they are, would but for this contrivance, be continually taking place.

Their Sail, which is a triangular Mat, is neatly rolled up upon this outrigger.

As Boki had sent on shore, intimating his arrival, to the highest personages of the place, we were in the afternoon visited by one of the inferior chiefs, and his wife, who was the daughter of Boki's nurse.

The man was rather an insignificant looking fellow, but his lady was a remarkably fine, portly dame. She came on board with only a cloth partly wrapped round her, and walked across the quarter deck, with a most stately disembarrassed air, to receive the salutations of the Captain, whose brows she graced with a chaplet of flowers, taken from her own person, and which constituted her only artificial ornament. She then went below, I suppose to chat over family concerns with Madame Boki. When she departed, the latter seemed to have given her peculiar directions respecting her negligent attire, as she reappeared, closely wrapped up in a Gown, given her by Madame Boki, and her former scanty wrapper, was handed over to the charge of her Attendants.

In the mean time, the Master and Surveyor returned on board, both agreeing in the practicability of bringing the ship into a very sheltered and secure anchorage, inside of the reef before alluded to, and about a mile distant from the Shore.

It was then determined that the Ship should return here to refit, but at present should proceed immediately to the seat of Empire, Woahoo [Oahu], it being highly necessary, that the regal bodies as well as those of the suite, should be first safely deposited on shore. We should then be enabled at our leisure to return to this place, to put the Ship in proper order. We therefore, in the evening, made the best of our way for Woahoo, previously intending to touch at the island of Mowee [Maui], in order to procure water, and also to have an interview with Kahumanu [Ka'ahumanu], the widow of the celebrated Tamehameha, a Woman possessing the highest authority in the island.

LO
great variety of trees"

At daylight we could distinctly perceive the lofty summits of Mowna Kaah [Mauna Kea], topping the clouds—its height entirely covered with snow—this mountain rises 16,000 feet above the level of the sea.—We soon saw the island of Mowhee, and throughout the day coasted along it, at the distance of about nine or ten miles from the land.

The scenery around appeared bold and rocky. The huts of the inhabitants were thinly dispersed along the shores, near which we perceived signs of Cultivation.

We also remarked here, as at Hido a great many beautiful waterfalls, descending precipitately, in foaming torrents from the lofty rocks, directly into the sea. These as we coasted along, produced a very novel effect. Towards the afternoon, we advanced near the place where we intended to anchor. At this time we were rapidly passing thro a channel, caused by the vicinity of the island of Ranai [Lanai] opposite to Mowee; here, an exceeding strong wind constantly prevails, and altho the water was as smooth as possible, we were carried on at the rate of 12 miles per hour. Shortly after we were entirely becalmed. Being at this time opposite the village of Lahaina, where we supposed the Queen Kahumanu was then residing, we fired a signal gun, which soon brought out several Canoes. One of the Natives came on board, from whom Boki learnt, that his Brother Karaimoku was excessively ill with a dropsical complaint, and that in consequence, all the principal Chiefs were assembled at Woahoo at which place the old Queen was also residing. We found however, that the young Princess "Nahienaena," sister of the little King, was then at Mowhee.

Boki, Madame Boki, and their August Suite, now prepared to pay their first return visit, and after some time spent in decking out their persons, they all appeared on deck clad in deep mourning. Madame Boki looked uncommonly engaging. She was dressed very smartly, and wore a fine black hat and feathers fit for the important occasion of receiving her naked relations. Boki did not at all seem to relish this first interview with his Countrymen, he expressed to Lord Byron his anxiety on the subject, and pointing to his stomach, said he felt something there, which indicated that all was not right. I suppose the sensation of fear affected him in this extraordinary manner.

However off they went, and the Officer who accompanied them, told me, that, as they neared the Shore, the Natives in some thousands were collected to receive them. Upon landing, a most loving scene of hugging, weeping, and rubbing of noses, took place, and they presently took their long absent Chiefs in their arms, and conveyed them to the house of Madame Boki's father [Hoapili], who is the greatest man in this island.

A slight Breeze shortly after sprung up, which enabled us to anchor immediately opposite the village, at about a quarter of a mile distant from the shore. It was now evening, Kuanoa [Kekuanaoʻa] the treasurer [of Liholiho's expedition to England] came off attended by a Chief of the island, intimating, that, on the following morning, the Natives would all assist in procuring us water, and the necessary refreshments of vegetables, Goats, and Pigs. As we found the surf would not allow us to send our Boats very close to receive the water, we were obliged to have recourse to the assistance of the Natives, who appeared to take great delight in filling our water casks, and floating them off to our sailors in the Boats.

In the course of the morning I went on shore with Lord Byron, and some of his Officers.

Boki, who was treated like a King, was upon the Beach to receive us. He conducted us along the seashore, surrounded on all sides by wondering Natives, to a large covered space, which was one of the King's storehouses. Here we found the young Princess, Madame Boki's Father, herself, and several Chiefs, together with an American Missionary, who acted as an interpreter.

The Princess is a little girl about 12 years old, not at all pretty, her face was quite disfigured by a large white Mob Cap, with which Madame Boki had shrouded her royal brows. She, as well as her immediate attendants, were clothed in black. On either side, were stretched out three or four fat huge looking chiefs on a sort of platform, covered with mats. Each chief wore, besides the maro [*malo*], a piece of stuff thrown over the left shoulder, hanging down very like the representations of ancient Roman dresses, their only occupation seemed that of lolling all day half asleep upon these mats, by which, with a suitable addition of Pig, and Poi, their persons become astonishingly corpulent.

Having thus far gratified my curiosity, I sallied forth to reconnoitre the village. It is composed of a vast number of huts, stretched along the shore upon a plain of three miles in extent, immediately beneath a high range of hills. This plain is in an excellent state of cultivation. The "taro" root upon which the natives principally subsist, flourishes in great abundance in fresh water ponds, planted round with Cocoanut trees. The breadfruit tree, and several others, the names of which I am ignorant, gave great beauty and interest to the scenery. In the midst of the village, is erected the Queen's house, which has the appearance of a nice English cottage. It was built by an American. Having found out a beautiful and characteristic spot, I immediately began a drawing. In an instant, I was surrounded by a vast number of Natives, all eagerly intent upon what I was committing to paper. They were all nearly naked, their behaviour was most orderly, & obliging, and if perchance, any of their companions placed themselves between me and the prospect I was delineating, they were instantly most unceremoniously hauled out of the way, and as each particular tree began to make its appearance, they evinced the greatest delight, pointing it out, and calling it by its country's name.

In order for my future sketches to see if they would submit to my drawing any of their persons, I persuaded two young ladies to stand before me, and having placed them in the most graceful attitudes, I began my design, and to my great delight, found that they were very patient and obedient during this tedious process. After I had quitted this spot, I sauntered about to see a little more of the village. The Inhabitants everywhere seemed delighted to see me. I entered into their huts, which I invariably found neat and tolerably clean. The ground is entirely covered with mats, and the houses are composed of reeds, and supported by strong poles, among which, are the Sugar cane, and Cocoanut tree branches, tastefully worked in, which add to their solidity, and compleatly prevent the rain from penetrating.

After having spent the greatest part of the morning on walking about, and viewing the Curiosities of the place, I returned on board in one of the Native's Canoes. These, notwithstanding their being so excessively narrow, are, on account of the Outrigger, uncommonly safe and commodious, and proceed thro' the water with astonishing celerity. The Natives on this island, appeared generally a well formed race of people, though not at all muscular or athletic. The women also are well made, tho they do not possess agreeable countenances. Our Chaplain informed me, that when on shore, the American Missionary had pointed out to him an Old Man, who had eaten part of Capt. Cook's heart. It appears, that after the unfortunate Officer had fallen a victim to the rage of the Natives, they, as is the custom with the remains of any great chief, divided the Body into several portions, with the intention of stripping the flesh from the Bones, which were carefully preserved, the heart, & entrails were destined to be burnt, and were hung up near a Morai [marae, or temple], for that purpose. Fate however ordered it otherwise—for the Old Fellow stole the heart, supposing it that of a Pig, and making off with his booty, ignorantly devoured it. Such is the story here:—? The Missionary at Mowhee speaks very favourably of the Natives conduct towards him. He has a comfortable house, and lands allotted to him, and receives a liberal salary from the Missionary board. He is married to one of his Countrywomen, who has accompanied him in his temporary banishment. In the afternoon, having received a supply of water, we weighed anchor & the little Princess, and several of the Chiefs came on board, in order to be conveyed to Woahoo, which we made early on the following morning.

As we were approaching the harbour of Honoruru [Honolulu] in this island, Mr. Charlton came off to receive us. From him we were glad to learn, that the news of our arrival had tended greatly to the improvement of Karaimoku's health, who was sufficiently strong to be enabled to sit up, and walk about a little. We shortly after came to an anchor, about two miles from the inner harbour of Woahoo. This place is an uncommon snug anchorage for small vessels, being close to the shore, and entirely protected on the sea side, by a Bar, which stretches itself out immediately before the town. Upon this bar, the Sea sometimes breaks most tremendously. The entrance for Vessels is very narrow. There is just sufficient depth of water over this bar, for our Frigate at high tide. We do not however like to venture in, as no ship approaching our size, has ever yet made the attempt.

We now fired a salute of 15 Guns, which was immediately answered by a fort from the town, as also from one on the heights, where, immediately overlooking the town is a strong natural battery, produced by the crater of an extinct volcano, upon whose summit, are planted several 32 pounders. These heavy guns form a grand protection for the town and harbour.

All our Sandwich friends proceeded on shore in the Ships pinnace, and Cutter, attended by two Officers, as also the Doctor, who was ordered to pay an immediate visit to Karaimoku. From the Surgeon, I learnt that a most formidable crowd had assembled to witness the disembarkation.

The little King, attended by a Body Guard of Sandwichers, armed with Muskets, was present at their landing, as likewise the Old Kahumanu who was drawn down to the Beach, in a sort of Pony chaise, or Dog cart, by eight harnessed natives. Immediately upon Boki's landing, the whole assemblage fell prostrate to the earth, from whence, after sundry groans and lamentations, the various Chiefs arose, and then performed their singular greeting of rubbing noses. I wonder Boki has any nose remaining, as so many kindred promontories have come into contact with it.—He then went to pay his visit of Ceremony to Karaimoku, the meeting I understand was very affecting between the two Brothers, who shortly after adjourned to a Church established here by the missionaries, and there returned their thanks to Providence, for the safe and happy return of the Chiefs to their Native Country.

As Lord Byron had determined not to make his triumphal entry, until the following day, we all remained on board. On that day Boki came to the ship, for the purpose of conducting us on shore, to be presented to Karaimoku, and the assembled Chiefs. He begged us all to clad ourselves in uniform, in order that the Ceremony might produce a more imposing effect. We set off in two Boats from the Ship. The Party consisted of his Lordship, two Lieutenants, Officer of Marines, and two midshipmen; then came the scientifics, the

Parson, the Naturalist, the Surveyor, myself as draftsman, and the Botanist.

Boki and Kuanoa, who attended upon us, were dressed in superb uniforms of Blue, turned up with red and gold lace, with long slashing basket hilted swords: lofty plumed cocked hats upon their heads, added to their natural sublimity. Immediately upon landing, the Fort fired a salute: as Karaimoku's house was about a quarter of a mile distant, we now arranged ourselves in marching order and surely, never could Roman General upon making his triumphal entry after a victorious campaign, have felt more on the occasion than our Friend Boki. First marched Lord Byron, one arm grasped by the far fam'd Governor, the other upheld by his majesty's epauletted Consul Mr. Charlton, then came the Lieutenants, Midshipmen, and scientifics, their arms all safely locked in those of sturdy Sandwich Chiefs, all clothed in black, who having arrived at the landing place, seized upon each luckless individual leaping from the Boat, as a companion in this grand & wonderous procession. Lastly came the sailors groaning under the weight of various presents allotted to the Chief Personages of this mighty Government. The road was tabooed, i e kept sacred, so that the Natives could not approach very near to us. Wonder and Curiosity were however depicted upon every Sandwich countenance, and as we silently tramped along, vast crowds on either side of the road were eagerly stretching forth their necks, in deep contemplation of their novel, and civilized Visitors.

We soon arrived at Karaimoku's house, which was the prepared seat of Audience. It was precisely like the huts, I before described, being simply a large covered space, floored with mats, and having three entrance doors. Here were assembled all the nobility of the different adjacent islands. At the head of the room were four Kahile's [*kahili*] (ensigns of royalty) composed of beautiful feathers of various colours, their shape bore great affinity of appearance, to a soldier's upright feather. Near these royal insignia, were seated on a sofa, covered over with cloaks, lined with scarlet silk Kaukiauli [Kauikeaouli], the young King, and the Princess Nahienaena. The Royal Youth is a common looking little fellow, and his regal skin was very much disfigured by a certain cutaneous disorder, not at all suitable to his dignified situation. On his left were seated Karaimoku and all the male Chieftains; on his right hand, Kahumanu, Riho Riho's widow [Kina'u], Mrs. Pitt, and many others, remarkable for their long names, hideous faces, & misshapen corpulent bodies. The women Chiefs, of whom were present about 30, were all dressed in black, each having a chaplet of feathers round their necks, as also a wreath encircling their heads. In the whole course of my life I never saw such an Assemblage, of disgusting looking creatures. With the exception of Karaimoku's wife there was not a tolerably goodlooking woman present. Some were as tall as their late Queen, all were disgustingly fat, and appeared very uneasy in their black silk dresses. The men were rather better looking. All however appeared awkward and uneasy in their English coats, and the absence of their native costume, very much destroyed the effect, which this scene would otherwise have exhibited. As it was however, the exhibition went off tolerably well.

Lord Byron was first introduced to Karaimoku, he then performed the ceremony of shaking hands with each fair dame in the congregation. We all followed his example. The presents were then brought forward; to Karaimoku was given on the part of our Sovereign, a handsome gold hunting watch, together with seals and chain. The Arms of England were engraved upon it. The widow of Riho Riho was then presented with a likeness of her deceased husband, engraved upon wax and encased in a gold frame. I narrowly watched Karaimoku, as he examined this picture. He seemed somewhat moved when contemplating it, and as it was handed to the disconsolate widow her feelings were also excited at the resemblance. As however she had lately married a young chief of the first rank, her grief very soon subsided, and in a few minutes more, she appeared as Gay as usual.

The next present was to Kahumanu. It consisted of a beautifully embossed silver teapot, with the Arms of England engraved upon one side, and on the opposite, her own name: this present seemed to give her the greatest satisfaction. It is rather surprising, that at this moment a rage prevails for possessing teapots, the whole Nation of Islanders, wishing to become determined Tea-drinkers. We now proceeded to unpack the little King's dress. It consisted of a very smart blue coat, richly embroidered with gold; to this was added a handsome cocked Hat and Feather, and to crown the whole, a magnificent sword was belted to his royal person. He seemed uncommonly pleased with this profusion of finery, and strutted about in great glee during the remainder of the day.

There are two American Missionaries in this Island, who are I think considering the infant state of civilization, almost too particular in their religious intercourse with the inhabitants. On Sundays, they will not allow the natives to cook their victuals, or take any inoffensive recreation. They also enforce their attendance on divine worship five times during the day. The consequence is, they are becoming daily in disrepute with the natives, who I should think, from such rigid examples, may conceive an austere and unfavorable notion of our Xtian religion. Moreover, they become tired by such unremitting assiduities in these ministerial vocations. One of these, a Mr. Bingham, the most methodistical looking gentleman, I ever beheld, placed himself near Karaimoku. On a sudden, he [Bingham] whispered something into the Minister's [Karaimoku's] ear, and immediately after said aloud, that it was Karaimoku's wish, that we should all join in prayer. Having therefore closed his eyes, and stretched forth his hands, he commenced an extemporaneous oration in English, which he bungled through in a canting, slovenly manner. He then gave his Audience a Stave couched in the Sandwich language, which seemed to slip from his tongue much more glibly.

After this ceremony, refreshments were brought. There is an old Spaniard in the island, named Marini [Marin], who talks English very well, and upon this occasion acted as our Interpreter. He is a sad old rogue, and from what I have heard respecting his character and conduct, has been guilty of every species of enormity. This man has managed to accumulate a considerable property in the island. He possesses a vast number of horned cattle, many horses, and mules, and has contrived to raise vineyards, from which he makes very tolerable wine. Fresh butter is also churned by the old Gentleman, and on the present important occasion, we were treated with the produce of his Farm.

The Company shortly afterwards dispersed, and we returned to our Ship, pretty well satisfied with our mornings introduction. I again visited the shore in the afternoon, and having procured a horse, took a ride further into the Country.

The town of Honoruru, the Capital of the Sandwich islands, is rather a considerable place: it is situated upon a plain, immediately at the foot of a high range of hills, and extends itself along the shore to the distance of about 3 miles.

The Town itself occupies about a quarter of this space. The habitations, with the the exception of a few houses erected by the Americans, are all built with straw, and very compactly put together; some of the best of them are very large, and capable of lodging fifty or sixty persons. These have three or four doors but seldom any windows. The interior space, there being no separation whatever, is covered with a profusion of mats, some of them frequently of a beautiful texture. The Chiefs occupy a sort of platform, raised about a foot from the ground, decked with the most beautiful mats, and their relations, friends, and dependents, herd indiscriminately around them. Very little attention has been paid in forming this cluster of huts into anything like a town or Village: here and there however, sufficient regularity has been observed to form a street or two. As a small piece of ground is generally attached to each house, encircled by a mud wall, or fence of long sticks, the Village has a straggling and irregular appearance. There are four or five decent looking houses erected by the Americans, one or two of stone, the others of wood; houses of the latter sort are brought in Framework from America. Karaimoku possessed a very large well built stone house, which he was just finishing as we arrived.

Immediately around the town, up to the very hills, the taro root, the principal food of the Natives, is cultivated in great profusion. This Plant which has a fine rich appearance, delights in swampy, marshy soil. The Springs from the Mountains are therefore turned into various channels, by which large patches of stagnate water are formed around the town: here the taro plant flourishes in great luxuriance.

There are also large salt water ponds formed immediately along the shore, and the vicinity of the Village. These are constantly well supplied with fish, on which, together with the taro, the Natives almost entirely subsist.

Near the shore, facing the entrance over the Bar into the inner harbour, is erected a very decent looking Fort, for a Sandwich Battery. It mounts about 40 Guns; these are of various Nations, and different calibres; they however form a warlike and civilized appearance when entering the harbour, which is completely protected by this formidable Fortification. In addition to these engines of defence, there is another Fort as before mentioned, on the top of a mountain which has the appearance of having been, at one time, an immense volcano. Here are mounted eight 32 pounders.

Our Salute being so promptly and regularly answered by these guns, rather astonished us. Upon all grand days, the Sandwich colours are hoisted upon the Forts. They are seven horizontal stripes, blue, red, and white, with the Union Jack at the corner. This forms one of the prettiest flags I ever saw, and is also well imagined, as indicating the union of the seven islands. Vessels of small burthen can lye very secure and close to the Shore, where there is a sort of pier formed, which facilitates their unloading. There were several ships lying in the harbour when we arrived: they were mostly American Whalers, who find this a convenient place for procuring refreshments, or putting their vessels in repair. These Islanders seem to have no idea of trade, in a general point of view, and they all appear very indifferent to the advantages which might redound to themselves, by establishing a commercial intercourse with other nations. Notwithstanding the fertility and teeming richness of the Soil, which, with very little care and industry, would produce Coffee, Cotton, and Sugar, in great abundance, they simply attend to the only article of commerce which nature spontaneously has afforded them. This is the Sandal Wood, which valuable commodity, is becoming more difficult to procure in any large quantity. The Chiefs having conceived, (and I believe very justly,) that the Americans have been constantly imposing upon them, by offering their goods at an exorbitant price, now demand themselves a ridiculously high price, not only for the Sandal Wood, but also for the necessaries for victualling the different ships, constantly arriving for this purpose.

At the time we arrived, they were actually requiring the sum of 10 dollars for a hog. Taro, yams, and other vegetables, were equally dear. The Americans, certainly, from the rapacity constantly practised by them, in their early commercial dealings with these people, richly deserve this severe retaliation. Ere we left the place, laws were established, regulating the price of provisions upon a more moderate footing.

On the 11th of May, it was decided, that the funeral should take place; great preparations were therefore making, to celebrate this momentous event. Two carriages, resembling light waggons, in which Kahumanu and other luxurious dames were wont to take the air stretched out upon their bellies, and drawn by six or eight Sandwichers, called *Kanaka*'s, were now befittingly appropriated for this mournful occasion. Four poles were erected at the corner of each of these vehicles, over which, folds of black tapa, the cloth of the country, were arrayed in decorous festoons. As no time had been allowed to erect a tomb, in which the Coffins might be deposited, Karaimoku prepared his own dwelling house for their reception, until a proper place should be built up.

This house, which was the same in which we were formally received, upon our first landing, was now converted into one of Mourning. Its walls and ceiling were entirely shrouded with black tapa, and in one corner was erected a platform of mats round which were hung curtains of the same lugubrious materials. This was destined to become the funeral bier of the royal Coffins.

Early on the morning of the 11th the bodies were taken from the hold and the Coffins uncovered. No expense seems to have been spared by our Government, in decorating these last frail tenements suitable to the rank of their unfortunate inmates. The Coffins were covered with very rich light crimson velvet, the Corners profusely

OAH

"Honoruru . . . at the foot of a high range of hill

R.D. delt 1826.

ornamented with appropriate gilded devices. On the top of each was a plate with the following inscription:

Kings Coffin

Tamehameha 2nd Elii
no nahina o awaii
make I Pelekani 28
Makaiki Kaiku I ke mahoe
mua o kemakaiki 1824
moa Ino no Komakou elii Iolani

Tamehameha 2nd King of the Sandwich Isles
died July 14 1824 in London in the 28 year of his age—
may we ever remember our beloved King Iolani

Queens Coffin

Tamahamalu Eli
no na haina o awaii
make I Pelekani 22
makaiki Taitu London 8
remahoe o re maraiki 1824

Tamahamalu
Queen of the Sandwich Islands
departed this life in
London
July 8, 1824
aged 22 years

All the boats were now put in requisition to assist in conveying to the Shore the Coffins and persons appointed to attend in the procession. I had previously left the Ship about two hours before these Boats, and being situated in Karaimoku's stone house, I could descry the range of Boats proceeding from the Ship in the following order.

First the Launch conveying the Coffins: next the Captain's Gig with himself and several Officers,—the Barge containing the company of Marines and band, after which followed the Pinnace and Cutter with the remaining Officers and Midshipmen. Each boat was provided with a flag hoisted halfmast high, and the Frigate, (also her colours thus adjusted,) began firing minute Guns from the time the Boats left her side. As the Coffins approached the Shore, the whole tide of noble blood in the island of Woahoo, hurried to the water's side, to take a part in the mournful office of attending the Coffins to the place where they were about to be deposited.

The King's guard was appointed to line the road through which the procession was to pass. They were all armed with Muskets but the appearance of their costume was highly ridiculous: they were all clothed in English dresses of various date, size, and manufacture, and many lacking in that essential part of a soldiers accoutrements, a pair of Trousers.

When a King dies, it is a custom, that none but Chiefs should assist at the funeral obsequies. In the present instance therefore, the Coffins being placed upon the Biers before described, were drawn by a number of the lower Chiefs. From the house in which I was seated, and around which the company had to pass, the Procession formed a most interesting and rather magnificent appearance. It was headed by nine Sandwichers accoutered in their beautiful war cloaks, each trailing along a huge feathered Kahile, similar to those I before described as being ensigns of Royalty: then came the Marine's their arms reversed, followed by the Frigate's Band playing Riho Riho's dead march, a solemn dirge composed for the occasion. After which martial Company proceeded the two American Missionaries clad in their gowns, with the Chaplain of the *Blonde* and the Surgeon. The Coffins then succeeded, dragged along by about forty chiefs all clad in deep mourning: these were closely followed by Lord Byron, the little King, and Princess, and all the Nobles of the land Male and Female, each having for a companion in this funereal Assemblage, one of the Officers of the Frigate. These were all clad in their dress uniforms, and certainly as they all tramped thus solemnly along, the whole group formed a striking and interesting Spectacle.

I could scarcely suppress a smile in viewing the enviable situation of some of my Friends, who, in addition to the quantity of dust and heat which constantly assailed them, had also the consoling obligation

VIRONS OF HONOLULU
he habitations . . . are all built with straw"

of supporting the immense inactive bodies of some of the Queens, who, unaccustomed to walk so far, complained grievously of this excessive exertion by the way of gratifying the manes of Riho Riho.

Kahumanu, as she leaned somewhat heavily upon the arm of our First Lieutenant, could not forbear exclaiming, (as she witnessed the regularity of the columns of legs and feet appertaining to the Marines,) "*Maitai*, *Maitai*," words denoting her royal approbation.

The Procession now passed along to the Church, which is a large thatched hut built similar to the dwellings around: here a part of the Funeral service was read over the Coffins, and they were then taken to Karaimoku's house. He, not being strong enough to walk in the Procession received the bodies at the door: they were then placed on the platform before mentioned; the Marines and whole body of mourners being drawn around, the band at the same time playing appropriate funeral airs. Thus ended this important ceremony: no Sandwich Prince has ever, or perhaps ever will again enjoy such magnificent sepulchral rites, & the event will no doubt form a grand æra in Sandwich history, whenever any Native historians shall spring up to celebrate it.

From what I understand, Riho Riho was not a Prince having the welfare of his kingdom at heart, notwithstanding his trip to England to procure laws to enable him to act and reign equitably. He was a great favorite with the people; the Chiefs however, considered him as an arbitrary and capricious ruler: He also degraded his kingly character by getting royally drunk. These Bacchanalian revels were constantly taking place, during which time, Guns from the Fort were regularly fired, immediately upon each bumper approaching the royal lips. During the Celebration of these disorderly rites, the King was wont to commit the greatest extravagancies, and opening the public treasures, lavished with unsparing hand considerable sums on his favorites and companions, in these disgraceful revels.

Tamamalu his wife bears an excellent character. She on the contrary was a universal favorite with all classes and the Natives seem universally to lament her death.

4 The Sandwich Islanders

A day or two after the funeral I commenced taking likenesses of the most important personages in the island. I had previously enquired of Kahumanu, the young Princess, and little King, if they would submit to the tedious operation of sitting for their Portraits. They all seemed highly delighted at this novel idea, particularly when I assured them that their pictures were to be shown to King George, for whom they all profess the highest veneration. I certainly did not anticipate that these savages would have given me so much trouble as they eventually did. In the outset I gave high offence to the haughty spirit of the mighty Kahumanu, for presuming to paint the young Princess before her; indeed, after I had actually begun the picture of the little girl, the old Lady stalked into the room full dressed, demanding that I should leave off the one I had already commenced, in order to practise upon her lowering countenance.

This was too much for my complaisance: certainly never Portrait Painter began his studies under less auspicious circumstances. The room,—the window of which I was obliged to close in order to obtain the most favorable light, became heated by the presence of a vast number of wondering lookers on, who, not contented with annoying me with their company, stalked about whistling, singing, spitting, and talking in so high a key, that my attention became quite distracted by this multiplicity of interruptions. Then their criticisms were equally agreeable. One would stretch out his hand immersing the tip of his finger in paint from my picture, declaring that I had given only one eye. Another complained that no hair appeared; it was in vain I represented to them the early stage of my picture, a gradual completion of which was quite beyond their comprehension.

I had also another difficulty to wrestle with. I wished my Friends to array themselves in their Country's Costume; this desire they treated as most unreasonable, and came decked out in their best black silk gowns, a fine characteristic dress to set off the graces of a tawny Sandwich islander. Despairing of reasoning my sitters out of their absurd prejudices, I confined my attention to their faces alone.

The little Princess sat uncommonly well, and I was enabled to make a very good beginning, with which she seemed highly gratified. She is a very well behaved little girl tho' somewhat plain.

Kahumanu having a very good wooden house, which had lately been brought from America, begged Lord Byron to take possession of it during his stay at Woahoo: On the 18th of May he became a resident there, and having invited myself, the Surgeon, Chaplain & Naturalist, to live with him, we passed our time very agreeably. We were amply provided with the greatest delicacies the island produced. Boki took care our Cuisine should be always well furnished; Marini the old Spaniard was ordered to supply us with new milk, butter and fruit, such as Grapes, Melons, Bananas, &c., and having our own cook and servants on Shore, we fared sumptuously every day.

In the mean time the Princess Nahienaena being unwell, I began the Portrait of the King Kaukiauli. His Majesty behaved tolerably well, and I contrived to make a pretty good likeness of him. His Attendants, a parcel of dirty half naked fellows annoyed me with their presence as usual. The Monarch himself kept me in continual alarm by his condescension and extreme affability, as his Royal body being covered with an active cutaneous disorder rendered it highly probable, that by frequent contact I might ultimately enjoy its irritating effects equally with himself. It required therefore my utmost ingenuity to keep him at arms length without betraying my disgust at his amicable approaches. This complaint (with us vulgarly called the "itch") is extremely prevalent here, it is quite melancholy to behold both men and women, perfectly formed and highly favored in every other degree, suffering from so loathsome and disgusting a disorder. Our Surgeon ascribes its prevalence to the quantity of raw fish and vegetable nourishment devoured by the Natives, which tend to impoverish the blood and render them subject to this disorder.

I had the honour of dining with this island Monarch two or three times: he gave me a dinner quite in the English style, and treated me (to them a great luxury,) with a few glasses of tolerable Port wine. His service of Plate not being in very good order, I presented him with a pair of new plated forks which pleased him amazingly.

I had now, a very important labour to undertake, that of painting the old Queen Kahumanu. As she had been notappointed [disappointed?] in my not commencing her portrait before the other two,

KAUIKEAOULI
"I began the Portrait of the King"

it now became my turn to entreat, and after attending upon her during a whole morning, and awaiting her final determination, she at last reluctantly consented to sit to me. As however I was about to commence, a vast objection was started. Being a tall fat woman of portly dimension, she wished a full length Portrait to be taken in order to give King George a good idea of her dignity and sublimity of appearance. I had only a half length canvass with me, upon which I endeavoured to point out to her the impossibility of crowding in her distended carcass. She sat down by no means contented with my explanation, and consequently exhibiting a countenance not altogether very pleasing.

It must be known that this Old Dame is the most proud, unbending Lady in the whole island. As the widow of the great Tamehameha, he possesses unbounded authority and respect, not any of which is she nclined to lay aside on any occasion whatever. To submit therefore o my will for an hour or two, was a severe trial to her pride, and her owering brow plainly indicated how derogatory to her dignity, were ny continual restrictions. Eager to get rid of so unpleasant a sitter, I astened on with my picture and soon finished her face, which was cknowledged by her Attendants as a most faithful likeness. As soon s the Old Lady perceived it she exclaimed with great vehemence, *oure maitai*" [very bad]—the truth was, I had committed to canvass er peculiar savage and stern look which is her natural expression f countenance. This repulsive look she generally contrives to conceal when in tolerable good humour, by assuming a most affected nile. On the present occasion however, she was too highly offended treat me with any of her winning graces—I now proceeded to her ostume, upon which point we fell out more than ever. She wished to gure in a fine black silk gown trimmed with lace, and I as obstinely required a piece of silk as drapery to be thrown over her shoulder ter the manner in which the Native tapa is worn.

My putting the Old Queen upon an equality with her subjects in oint of dress, again aroused her slumbering indignation. She however sat down, but just as I was about to rub in the folds of the drapery, e suddenly rolled off the chair upon the ground, where she lay on her Belly (the usual royal posture,) declaring that part to be

NAHI'ENA'ENA
"The little Princess sat uncommonly well"

affected with dolorous pains, and vowing she would sit no longer. I therefore determined to finish the portrait without further consulting the whims and fancies of so capricious a sitter.

During the mornings and evenings I generally took a walk, both to make sketches and also to procure an insight into the manners and customs of the Natives. The heat in the middle of the day rendered any exertion extremely fatiguing and unpleasant, particularly in a country where there are scarcely any trees to protect one from the Sun.

The natives of the Sandwich islands may justly I think be considered a well formed race of people. The men are rather above the middle size, and tho' neither robust or muscular, are active, strong, and from what I beheld capable of great exertion and fatigue. I saw very many amongst them whose persons would have formed unexceptionable models for the most fastidious sculptor. Their skin is of a fine copper colour, tho in a few instances I have seen them almost as dark as an African Negro. Their countenances, generally speaking, are by no means agreeable. They possess very quick eyes, the vivacity of which gives a sort of restless ferocity to the general expression of their faces. They have very fine white teeth, tho they are in the habit of disfiguring their mouths by extracting four or five of their front teeth, as commemorating the death of any deceased hero. Since the death of Tamehameha, this barbarous custom has been fast disappearing, and poor Riho Riho's manes must have been gratified with a very insignificant number of grinders, when compared with the sufferers at his Father's decease.

Their hair is of a shining black, either curly or straight as the inclination is perceptible with us, from their constantly being in the water. However, it is coarse and frequently of a tawny colour; they stain the roots of it with lime, which turns it white and gives a very peculiar appearance to the countenance. Some wear it extremely long: flowing down their backs. Others tie it up so as to form a plume on the top of the head. Again it is the fashion to cut it extremely short on each side of the head, giving it the appearance of a Dragoon's helmet.

They are fond of tatooing their bodies, the favorite places upon which they operate are the insides of the arms, legs and thighs, where are exhibited devices of all descriptions. I have seen some of them with one half of the Body thickly tatooed so as to appear of a dark blue colour, the remaining half is left in its original state. They also design Cows, Goats, and other animals on their foreheads and cheeks.

The men appear entirely naked with the exception of the "maro" a piece of tapa passed between their thighs, which is brought up and fastened on the hips.

In cold weather, and when not actively employed, they wear another piece of tapa which, tied in a loose knot depends from the right shoulder after the manner of the Roman toga, and forms the most graceful mass of drapery imaginable. The women do not I think possess that sweetness and sensibility of countenance ascribed to them by Cook, I scarcely ever beheld a pretty girl. They however in general are most beautifully formed. Some possess the most exquisite symmetry of shape: nothing could exceed the charming contour of their arms, legs, ankles and feet. Added to these Attractions, they have a graceful manner of using these beautiful limbs, thus void of ligature, stay, and other embarrassment attendant upon the dress of an English Belle. They wear their hair extremely long flowing down their backs.

The dress of the women consists of a piece of Tapa which is called a Pow [*pa'u*]; this being passed round the waist is tucked in at the ends, and hangs down just below the knees; they also, like the men, have another piece of Tapa, which at night, or in cold weather, they make use of as a shawl. Both sexes are uncommonly fond of ornamenting their persons, and evince a great deal of taste in forming chaplets of flowers and wreaths for their heads and necks. These chaplets are remarkably pretty; they are made by stringing a number of flowers plucked closely from the stalk upon a piece of grass or small creeper. These they arrange upon their heads in the most tasteful manner. The Colours most in Fashion are yellow, orange, and crimson flowers, which appear to be cultivated solely for this purpose; their necks are also frequently encircled with wreaths of leaves. Most of the "Females" possess a small looking Glass which they are very fond of consulting.

Whilst I was painting Kahumanu's picture I was every instant interrupted in order that she might contemplate her features in a small mirror which hung beside her. Only the Chiefs appear clothed in European dress; even then on great days the large yellow feathered wreaths are constantly worn by the Female Chiefs.

The Superb feathered cloaks, tippets, and helmets, are now completely laid aside. They however form a very excellent article of traffic, and the Islanders can hardly be induced to part with them, except at a very high price.

From what I perceived of the character of the people, I should say they are blest with the most mild and tractable natures possible. The Chiefs possess unbounded sway over them; their will is a perfect law. To us they were at all times civil and obliging, tho' they never felt inclined to exert themselves particularly, except when our commands were enforced by the authority of a Chief. Thus ordered, they would undertake anything for us. They begin now to understand the value of money, and are no longer willing to barter for beads or insignificant trinkets. We constantly had plenty of traffickers about the house of the old Queen, bringing Idols, Shells, Stone axes, and other Curiosities, for which they invariably demanded a dollar.

Observing that several of us were eager to possess some of these ancient Idols they diligently set to work, and soon fabricated a great number of grim looking deities. To these they endeavoured to give as ancient a look as possible hoping thus cunningly to impose upon our credulity.

Some of the higher Chiefs have amassed together considerable sums of money, which they most unprofitably conceal under ground: there is a Cave at OWhyhee in which is deposited the royal treasure, as also large sums belonging to Kahumanu. The precise situation of this Cave is only, I believe, known to one family in that island: to be found near its precincts is a Capital crime, and instantaneous death is inflicted upon the luckless offender.

The Government appears uncommonly simple: All their lands belong to the King, who divides it to his several Chiefs to be enjoyed by them during his lifetime. This enables him to make any demands on their possessions he pleases. Again the Chiefs parcel their lands out to the common people, who undertake to till, and keep them in order, that they may procure their daily food. They can, however, boast as possessing nothing of their own, and are liable at any time to have their huts and possessions taken from them, and themselves most capriciously abused.

If they are not contented with their present Chiefs, they are allowed to change masters as often as they please. Notwithstanding this arbitrary mode of Government, I should say that these people are perfectly happy, their wants are very few. Nature has supplied them with a soil abundantly prolific, and which requires scarcely any labour to keep in constant cultivation. Their habitations are all built in a day; from trees they are furnished with clothing, canoes, and implements of husbandry—and their Fish ponds, taro patches, yams, &c., amply supply them with every luxury a Sandwicher can possibly wish for.

They evince great ingenuity in various mechanical arts. Their canoes are uncommonly well constructed. Formerly a stone axe was the only instrument employed in chiselling them out. They at present make use of the English adze which considerably facilitates the operation of hollowing their canoes. They make very beautiful bowls from a fine hard wood of the Country. The Cocoanut tree supplies them with excellent materials for forming good cords of every dimension; its fruit presents to them drinking cups, & musical instruments.

The Bark of this tree [*wauke*, or paper mulberry] is converted into an excellent sort of cloth, and various berries form a beautiful dye for producing the colours: yellow, orange, purple, and red, the most prevalent colours for their tapa's.

The Bark of the tree is beaten out upon large blocks of wood with infinite labour; after being rendered sufficiently thin, various devices are printed by means of small slips of cane, the ends cut into different patterns, which, being dipped in the dye are carefully prest upon the cloth—this is a tedious operation, but it is performed with great ease and regularity.

Nothing astonishes a stranger more than their curious manner of testifying their grief for their deceased friends: when any death takes place in a Family, all the relations assemble together, and commence a

loud and monotonous wailing for several hours together. Should a Chief have departed this life, a large Band of these Mourners are hired to perform at his funeral obsequies. They evince the utmost heartlessness on such occasions, and during fits of apparently most excessive grief, will stop, laugh and talk to a passer by, and then again proceed with their doleful lamentations.

On the 23rd an operation took place the contemplation of which some days previously had put the whole island in a ferment. The state of Karaimoku's health since our arrival, had been gradually becoming worse, and our Surgeon conceived that the only chance left for him was that of submitting to be tapped. To this the poor sufferer willingly consented; a day therefore having been appointed, Lord Byron accompanied by one of the lieutenants, & the Doctor, proceeded to the Minister's house.

The surrounding Chiefs seemed much astonished and affected at what appeared to them our hazardous experiment, and Kahumanu frequently shed tears as the instrument and Apparatus were preparing. Lord Byron having a bandage ready, attended upon the Surgeon's movements, who, owing to the old Gentleman's extremely tough hide, found great difficulty in perforating his stomach. Having at length accomplished this, he drew from his patient a considerable quantity of Water which afforded him almost instant relief.

This simple Operation seems to have produced upon the minds of the Chiefs the most perfect astonishment; they could not at all understand that it was possible for a man to exist after a hole had been made in his belly, which is considered with them the Seat of Life. One of them indeed asked Lord Byron if the Minister's breakfast of Poi would not issue through the aperture.

Thus happily ended this important and successful undertaking, the failure of which might have been attended with unpleasant consequences. Marini assured the Doctor that he had heard, that had Karaimoku expired during the time the Operation was performing, the Doctor's life would certainly have paid the forfeit of his temerity and unskilful performance.

The truth of this Assertion is much to be doubted; as it was, this cure tended very much to our celebrity.

A YOUNG HAWAIIAN CHIEFESS
"I selected . . . a girl . . . uncommonly well formed"

The good effects of these Æsculapian experiments were quickly perceptible in the person of Karaimoku, whose health from the tapping day gradually improved—the swellings about his legs quickly disappeared, and ere we left Woahoo he was completely relieved from the baneful effects of his disorder.

In the mean time I continued busily employed in sketching and taking portraits, and having finished all the royal members of the August house of RihoRiho, I proceeded to search for less noble, but more interesting subjects for my pencil. I selected a boy & a girl, both uncommonly well formed and possessing agreeable countenances who for a small compensation allowed me to take their Portraits arrayed in their Native Costume. They both sat well, and altho engaged in this manner for three or four days, they betrayed not the slightest degree of impatience, but appeared quite elated at the honour I was conferring upon them. We now began to prepare for our departure for Hido, where it was determined the Ship should be refitted.

The more I beheld of the Sandwich Chiefs the less I felt inclined to admire them. I frequently paid Karaimoku a visit and generally found him sitting only in his shirt surrounded by his wives and the different Queens, all stretched out upon mats lying on their bellies, and resembling a litter of Gigantic Pigs.

The Chiefs and Kanaka's in point of bodily appearance, seem quite another race of people. The former, especially the women, owing to the inactivity of their lives arrive at a degree of Corpulency quite revolting. There is one delicate Queen measuring about six feet one inch in stature, and weighing about 23 stone [322 pounds].

Nothing gave me a greater disgust at these people than their manner of eating. Several large Calabashes of Poi appear well filled: this constant accompaniment to a Sandwich feast is made from the Taro root, which after being boiled, is pounded beween two large stones, until, by the addition of a small quantity of water it assumes the appearance of a very thick paste. It is then put aside for a day or two, and by allowing it to ferment it acquires a tart taste. It then undergoes another pounding, after which it may be pronounced ready for consumption. This food is the universal standby, and it seems hardly

A YOUNG HAWAIIAN CHIEF
"... a boy ... quite elated at the honour"

possible for a Sandwicher to exist without his Calabash of Poi. They assert that it is exceedingly fattening. In order therefore to be benefitted by its good effects, I generally took a portion every morning; by adding Milk and Sugar it may be rendered very palatable, and thus seasoned, has the taste of Gooseberry fool.

Several large Calabashes of this excellent food having been thus prepared each member of the feast protrudes his or her two forefingers into the bowl, to these, by a circular motion being made, a large portion of Poi adheres sufficiently firm to allow the loaded members to carry their booty to the mouth. After having sucked them clean, they proceed to another dive, and it is quite astonishing to observe with what dexterity and dispatch a large bowl of Poi disappears owing to these frequent immersions. They also at the same time provide themselves with a quantity of raw fish, to which is added a sort of seaweed by way of sauce, bearing the most rank, fishy disagreeable smell imaginable. The heads of the fish, gills, liver, &c., are set apart by themselves, & considered great delicacies.

The first time I beheld this loathsome mixture, from its sanguinary hue, I mistook it for a bowl of red fruit thus mashed up.

Dogs also are considered by a Sandwich Epicure as forming a delicious dish, and as such one would conceive they were particular in their manner of rearing their canine food: on the contrary they are generally half starved and are allowed to feed on offal, putrid fish, & any other tit morsel that may fall in their way, so that the flesh of a wholesome English dog would be infinitely preferable.

When doomed to be devoured, they generally strangle them. I have seen several about to be baked, their hair all peeled off, the eyes starting from the sockets, with a grim snarl shewing the white grinders & thereby giving the animal so ghastly an expression, that none but determined dog devourers, would dare partake of so horrible a meal. It is also surprising that dogs are great favourites when alive; the natives take them in their arms, & not unfrequently, condescend to treat them with Poi from their own mouths.

Most of the chiefs still adhere to this delicious food; Madame Boki however, whom I frequently visited has begun to lay aside in a great measure these uncivilized repasts. She no longer has her meals served up without Plates, knives & forks, &c., but spreads her table cloth, & directs her table to be laid out in English fashion.

Boki, since his return, has become very much liked; he is quite a new man. Formerly, like his chieftain brethren, he was as slothful & indolent as any of them. He now attends to the tillage & cultivation of his lands, assists Karaimoku in the government of the islands, & by his affability & kindness, has become a great favourite with the Kanakas.

At the death of his brother, he will no doubt assume the Regency without opposition.

Madame Boki, since her return from England, has acquired an excessive passion for dress and finery. It is quite ridiculous to observe how very attentive she has become to the minutiae of her toilette. She never appears in dishabille, notwithstanding so many naked examples constantly surrounding her, but still wears her English stays, braces herself in, & assumes all the airs of a fine lady amongst her less favored countrywomen.

I have seen her making a round of visits, to her sister chiefs, dressed out in the height of English fashion, with Parasol, Leghorn bonnet, & satin shoes. Her fair female friends are I think rather envious of her decorative accomplishments, & Kahumanu has already begun to regard her with an evil eye, as also her husband Boki, whom she mortally detests.

I attended a few days ago a meeting of the chiefs to deliberate on the education of the young King. Many wise & salutary counsels were recommended by the various chiefs. At last Boki rose up, & after speaking of the loyal & dutiful behaviour of the subjects of England to their monarch, acknowledged his affection for his youthful Prince, & concluded his speech by affirming, that if all the bellies of the assembly felt as his did towards his King, they would be a loyal set of subjects indeed. This manner of speaking of the affection of the belly (which with this people is a universal saying) will put one in mind of Scriptural language as "the yearning of the bowels."

A few days before our departure for Hido, Lord Byron gave an entertainment on board, to the King, Karaimoku, & the different chiefs male & female. They attended arrayed in their most costly

European finery, & expressed great approbation at the size of the ship, its (to them) astonishing conveniences, & the pleasant and liberal manner in which they were treated. Indeed his Lordship, by his affability & good management has completely won the affections of these goodnatured islanders. The King and August suite were much gratified by a salute being fired on their leaving the ship.

I had forgotten to mention that horses had been introduced some time since to these islands: many of the chiefs possess them and when I felt inclined to ride, I petitioned the young King to lend me one of his stud; which he very readily granted. The mountains however, rise so abruptly immediately behind this plain of Honoruru, that you are unable to proceed far from the place on horseback; I therefore generally preferred sauntering about in order to become more acquainted with the inhabitants.

These people in general possess very little curiosity, even the sight of the whole of the paraphernalia belonging to a Frigate, produced upon them little or no emotion. I however had in my possession an instrument, which upon being displayed, invariably brought a wondering & delighted crowd around me: this was no other than a common walking stick which I was enabled by unfolding to convert into a seat. At sight of this simple piece of machinery, upon which I always sat when taking my sketches, I invariably drew sixty or seventy people about my person, and the approbationary exclamations of "*Mayti Mayti*" [*maika'i maika'i*] were continually bursting forth from all sides. I therefore became very well known in the village, & was designated by the title of Pala pala, which in their language signifies writing or drawing, both being synonomous with them. The natives are inveterate mimics. I once found one of them armed with my pallet & mahlstick pretending to be busily engaged in painting, & running to & fro with a face of well feigned anxiety, he appeared as just putting the finishing touches to my picture.

They have several games: one or two are practised with balls, something like our own schoolboy exercises. Another very favourite amusement with them is, throwing a circular stone about three or four inches in diameter, & two of thickness: this, with an underjerk they propel along a narrow path with most astonishing velocity.

I have seen an active man give a sufficient impetus to one of these stones to cause it to roll about two or three hundred yards. They are also most expert swimmers, and pass a great part of their time in the water: they have a favourite aquatic amusement, which is very entertaining to behold. A man having a large flat board, about a foot & one half broad, & eight or ten in length, places himself on its surface, at some little distance from the shore, & awaiting a good opportunity, (his care being always to select the largest wave) laying himself along the board & using his hands as paddles, he rides securely to the beach, being propelled forwards by a wave, immediately before which, his care is to direct his surf board. In this manner by keeping the surf board end on, (as sailors say) they proceed thro' the water with astonishing celerity.

I have been in a canoe when the natives paddling her have performed the same feat: the wave rolled foaming close on our stern, the natives taking care to keep their flying canoe exactly in a line with their precipitate pursuer: this experiment in a heavy surf, must be a nervous undertaking.

Altho the natives are constantly immersing their bodies in the briny wave, still I am concerned to say, that very few are exempt from having their head quarters taken possession of by a most noisome band of invaders. The forbearance on their parts in thus giving protection & support to such detestable colonies, is certainly loathsome enough, what then will be said when I assert, that I have frequently seen these clean people as Cook denominates them, searching each others heads for these capital intruders, which when pounced upon, are invariably devoured by the successful finder.

I have even seen children perform this delectable operation upon the sconces of their parents, dutifully offering each hapless visitant, as it gradually arrived within grasp of forefinger & thumb.

The Queens I believe are exceptions to this disgusting practice, indeed they are very careful in keeping their heads and persons constantly clean & uncontaminated. But I hasten to pass by such disgusting scenes, & am almost ashamed to have allowed them a place in the hitherto pure & unsullied sheets of my journal, the characteristic features & habits of a nation ought however to be faithfully delineated.

It being known that we were about to sail for Hido, Kahumanu, greatly to his Lordship's dismay, requested him to take her in the *Blonde* to this place. To this he assented begging however that she would not burden his ship with too numerous a retinue.

On the 7th therefore, which was the day appointed for sailing, the old lady came on board attended by a Queen her sister, two or three under chiefs, &, notwithstanding his Lordship's injunctions, a retinue of about forty half clad Kanakas accompanied the old dame. She also brought two large chests, in one of which was a considerable sum of money destined to be deposited in the cave at Hido. Added to these were a vast quantity of raw fish & Poi. This accumulation of naked natives, proved vastly disagreeable: the main deck became the head-quarters, & the variety of stenches produced from the raw fish, sour Poi, &c., were quite overwhelming. Kahumanu and her sister took possession of a part of the fore cabin, which was skreened off for their convenience. When the old lady came on board, her first question was addressed to our first Lieutenant, demanding the number of Guns with which she was to be saluted.

As a salute was decreed to her, she sat on the quarter deck, enjoying with a triumphant look, so much noise, powder & smoke all redounding to her honour. I do not at all admire the character of this royal personage, she appears haughty, proud & vindictive, and formerly her power was marked with acts of a most sanguinary nature. It is said that not long since detecting a young urchin secretly making game of her, she became so enraged, that suddenly pouncing upon the luckless offender, she with one mighty whirl dashed his brains out against a neighbouring wall. Of late years the missionaries have effected a great deal in subduing & restraining this impetuous spirit. As it was, she was no favourite with any of us, indeed, she scarcely deign'd to notice any but Lord Byron; even he was sometimes treated with coldness & disdain.

We now bade farewell to our friends at Woahoo. Boki appeared much concern'd to part with us; as he had victualled the ships company from his own estate, during the time we had been here, Lord Byron paid him about 700 Dollars on this account, which at first he was very unwilling to accept. I believe that our government had directed that all supplies for the ships use should be punctually paid for.

The conduct of Boki is extremely unlike that of the other chiefs, whose insatiable avarice is quite remarkable: they lose no opportunity of adding to the secret hoard of Dollars they all more or less possess, & which is generally carefully concealed underground.

5 Return to Hilo

From the 7th until the 12th we were beating up against a strong trade wind to Hido, all uncomfortable, & anxious to get rid of our royal charge & suite. After having been laying about a month at the dangerous & exposed harbour of Woahoo, above two miles from the shore, & the passage without attention rendering boats liable to be swamped, (we had one boat upset,) from the heavy surf constantly rolling in, it may be imagined how delighted we all were, upon arriving at a spot so very different in every respect.

Hido may most appropriately be termed the Valparaiso of the Sandwich Islands. The view from the ship, a panoramic drawing of which I have taken, is peculiarly striking.

On all sides the most lively verdure prevails, luxuriant breadfruit trees flourish to the water's edge; these are thickly intermingled with towering cocoanut trees; amongst these are scattered the neat looking huts of the natives. In the distance the gigantic forms of Mowna Kaah, & Mowna Roa [Mauna Loa], rear their towering crests to the clouds; the summits of the former are continually veiled in snow, & the eye, wandering from the sunny landscape below, enjoys a fine contrast when resting on the bleak & snow capt peaks of the neighbouring mountains.

At five on the following morning I rose to go on shore. A sunrise at this place, is the most beautiful thing in nature I ever beheld: the tops of Mowna Kaah, & Mowna Roa, become a complete mass of the most lively crimson, their tints rendered more vivid & brilliant by the cold grey morning mists in which the woods & country at their base are thickly enveloped. I hastened on shore, & was much gratified with my morning's excursion & amusement. We landed at the mouth of a beautiful fresh water stream, which empties itself into the sea, & along whose meandering banks, shaded by cocoanut and breadfruit trees, we pursued our walk until we came to a large reservoir, which had been formed for the purpose of rearing & keeping fish.

As we went further into the country, we saw several of these ponds, which we afterwards understood belonged to Kahumanu, who indeed possesses a vast extent of land at Hido.

All these lakes are most plenteously stocked with very fine fish, resembling mullet, which, taken from the neighbouring streams, are fed & fattened here, & flourish so abundantly, that a native assured me, (I am not prepared to back his veracity by ocular demonstration) that he once tumbled into one of these ponds, and was literally buoyed up by the immense quantity of fish immediately beneath him. Still no Kanaka is allowed to touch them, indeed before our arrival, the two missionaries who are stationed here, could scarcely ever procure any. For us however, to whom in point of furnishing provisions, they have been at all times abundantly liberal, orders were immediately issued to draw the ponds, & during our stay here we had a constant supply of these excellent fish, daily furnished for our tables.

Owing to the woods being uncommonly thick, together with the rugged stratas of Lava, which everywhere abound in this neighbourhood, we were unable to extend our walk very far; we were however altogether amazingly pleased with the appearance of the country, & congratulated ourselves in having so snug a place to refit the ship in. Her rigging underwent in a very short time a thorough overhauling. In the mean time Lord Byron having expressed a wish to Kahumanu that he should like to live on shore, she accordingly assigned to him a large & commodious habitation which had just been built for one of the chiefs.

This house was most agreeably situated on the banks of the stream, I before mentioned: the floor which was strew'd with small pebbles was carefully covered with mats. It had two doors & several windows & when stocked with a few chairs & a table, presented to us a very original & comfortable dwelling place.

I was again kindly invited to live with his Lordship, as well as the surgeon, naturalist & chaplain. We all brought our cots on shore, & suspended them from the corners of the house; in this as in all their dwellings there was no partition. His Lordship had therefore a part skreened off with Tapa for his bedroom.

Every thing being thus arranged, we entirely deserted the ship, & I do not know when I have spent my time so delightfully, as during the three weeks we sojourned at this place.

Kahumanu ordered several houses to be erected for herself & suite, immediately in the neighbourhood of our own. Her commands were most promptly executed, & in the course of four & twenty hours three or four huts reared their pigmy heads. These notwithstanding the dispatch were well & firmly built. They were roofed & lined with banana and the broad thick leaf of the tea [ti] plant, and thus rendered completely impenetrable from rain for at least two months. After that time the leaves become devoured by insects which breed in them, & the hut then requires a new covering. Our habitation was roofed & lined with the leaf of the Pandanus tree, which will last, and completely defy the inclemency of the weather, for six or seven years.

Lord Byron brought with him a native from Woahoo, who could speak English, & was called Sir Joseph Banks, a most active and ingenious fellow: this man became our purveyor, and being delegated with supreme authority by Kahumanu, commenced supplying the ship with every description of refreshment most abundantly.

It was astonishing to perceive with what duty & reverence the people looked upon Kahumanu. Her will was a perfect law. The whole property of the Kanakas at Hido was at her disposal, & therefore notwithstanding the old dames airs and vagaries, we considered it both wise & political to make ourselves as agreeable & amiable as we possibly could. Her manners & conduct were so much improved, since her former residence at Hido, which she had not revisited since her husband Tamehameha's death, that she was now designated by the inhabitants, the good Kahumanu. She has become exceedingly attentive to her religious duties, & never misses an occasion of going to church or meeting.

Upon seeing Mr. Ruggles, one of the American missionaries here, she took him by the hand & said: "When I formerly was in the habit of seeing and conversing with you, I then hated you, I now love & esteem your character." Both the missionaries were delighted with this visit from the old lady. They hope her conduct towards them, & attention to religious duties, will have a good influence over the minds of the inhabitants, who are not particularly well inclin'd towards them.

All our supplies at this place, which consisted of fish, Poultry, yams, Pigs, Taro, plaintains, &c., were furnished gratis, & without any difficulty whatever. Our indefatigable purveyor, backed with the all powerful name of Kahumanu, provided for our wants at a moment's notice.

I amused myself during the time I remained here, in making as

WAIAKEA RIVI

"The natives are constantly in the wate

R.D. delt. 1826.

many sketches as I possibly could: altho the scenery was beautiful, still it possessed little variety, & owing to the very difficult walking, sharp lava rocks springing up in all directions, it was tedious & fatiguing to advance into the country, added to which Hido is a notorious place for rain, which sometimes proved uncomfortable & inconvenient.

One recreation here was particularly delightful, which was that of bathing in the fresh water stream before our door. I generally indulged myself in this refreshing exercise two or three times a day: the natives are constantly in the water, & it was at all times a curious and novel sight to see so many people of both sexes, constantly sporting about in this refreshing element, & exhibiting a variety of tricks. They were very fond of walking with their hands along the bottom of the river, showing only their feet & legs above the surface of the water. I have seen two or three dozen pairs of legs thus exhibited, making their way gradually across the stream. They are particularly expert in swimming, and delight in throwing themselves into the water from very great heights.

About a mile & a half from our hut, situated on the opposite side of the bay, was a most beautiful waterfall, which, descending from a ledge of Lava rocks, emptied its contents into the sea. Nothing can be more romantically picturesque than the situation of this delightful spot: it proves a most excellent watering place for ships, whose boats are enabled to enter a small creek, & take in their water immediately below the falls.

The entrance is rather wide & easily approached. On either side are high precipitate rocks whose brows are ornamented with cocoanut and breadfruit trees. The sides of these rocks are covered with beautiful creepers of all descriptions, abundantly bearing flowers of every hue & dye, & large elegant spreading leaves almost conceal the rock itself from your view. Having advanced about one hundred & fifty yards, you arrive at the first fall, beyond which the boats are unable to proceed. A few yards higher up is a grander & more important fall, descending from a ledge of black lava rocks.

The scenery around is strikingly beautiful. In company with Lord Byron, I frequently of an afternoon took a paddle across the bay, in a small double canoe which was always at his command, in order to witness the aquatic sports of the natives, who were very fond of exhibiting their dexterity at this place. I have seen several plunge in above the fall, & allow themselves to be transported down by the roaring torrent which tumbled them over a precipitate ledge of rugged lava rocks, into a foaming abyss below. One would suppose when approaching this place, that they were incurring the risk of being dashed to pieces: the exercise however seems to afford them the greatest diversion. Overwhelmed by the whirling eddies they for a few moments entirely disappear then soon rise at some distance from the first fall, & are ready to encounter the second which however is inconsiderable when compared with the first.

I have also seen some of the natives place themselves on the brow of a cliff, its height being about fifty feet, & with a running leap precipitate their persons into the fall below. These feats, both men and women and even children are fond of practising, & appear pleased at the astonishment excited in us at witnessing such daring adventures.

Shortly after our arrival at Hido some of our officers undertook a journey to the top of Mowna Kaah: they found this a most difficult and fatiguing enterprise. They were obliged to make their way thro almost impassable woods. Sometimes they were forced to cross torrents & rocky ravines, and at last when arriving at the dreary summit of all their wishes, so thick a haze prevailed, that the boundless prospect seen from so exalted a height in fair weather, was completely shrouded from their view. In a clear day, from the top of this mountain, most of the islands composing the Sandwich group, are distinctly discernible. The party returned after a week's absence, disappointed, & almost worn out by fatigue.

Lord Byron had now an undertaking in contemplation; that was of paying a visit to the celebrated Paley [Pele, Kilauea] volcano. As the fulfilment of this exploit was attended with most terrible difficulties, I cannot forbear giving a minute description of so arduous an undertaking. Lord Byron possessing such influence with the powerful Kahumanu, was determined to perform his journey in the most commodious luxurious manner possible: he had sometime before received a severe wound on his leg from the kick of a horse at Woahoo;

YRON BAY, HILO
Romantically picturesque"

as this was not yet healed, he determined to make this journey in a litter.

Kahumanu undertook to provide a sufficient number of natives to carry our baggage &c., & to assist us in our encampments. Moreover she ordered two houses to be built for our convenience on the road. Our journey was computed to be about forty miles distant, the road uncommonly bad, & a great deal of uphill to prove our perseverance & good wind.

Our party was to consist of Lord Byron, our first Lieutenant, myself, surgeon, chaplain, naturalist & surveyor, together with two midshipmen. The two American missionaries also volunteered to accompany us.

Each person took his hammock & a few changes of raiment, & Lord Byron provided all eating necessaries, cooking utensils, and a proper quantity of wine, brandy & Porter. On monday morning on the 22d. our forces having assembled at five o'clock, after swallowing a hasty breakfast, we prepared to depart: about 200 *Kanakas* attended upon us to carry our baggage &c. and a chief was dispatched to assist us in the management of so many natives. About twenty young ladies also voluntarily offered to accompany & assist us.

Thus prepared & attended, we all set off with light hearts & thick shoes, little dreaming of the labours & difficulties we were about to encounter. The first five or six miles were trod over with a light foot. The path, tho unpleasant from the uneven & projecting points of Lava, upon which we were constantly stumbling, was nevertheless quite beautiful when compared with our subsequent vile road.

Having gone thus far we halted at the verge of a very thick wood, for the purpose of augmenting our supply of water as we were given to understand that we should not be enabled to replenish our vessels with this precious fluid, until we had walked seven or eight miles. As we approached the wood, I was particularly struck with the beauty of the various trees forming its skirts; the principal was the Ti [*kukui*] tree, from which the natives procure a species of nut, which being baked & strung in rows upon sticks, answer the purpose of candles. Our path as we struck into the wood became very bad; moreover a spirit of pedestrian emulation spreading throughout the party, each member violently hurried on, in spite of all local oppositions.

Our path presented to us one continual mass of lava rendered extremely dangerous by pointed rocks, rents, & projecting ridges, covered with long grass & creepers; added to this a great quantity of rain having fallen in the morning, each step, as you were obliged to leap from rock to rock, became exceedingly precarious & fatiguing. So sharp and rugged were these inveterate stones, that in a short time, hardly one of the party could boast of a sound shoe. The heat also proved excessively oppressive. I kept floundering along as well as I was able, most sincerely envying the disembarrass'd state of a pair of well turned legs, skipping along immediately before me. These belonged to one of the female attendants of our train, who seemed to make very light of the bad & uneven road. She frequently turned, & rather maliciously seemed to enjoy my sufferings. Determined not to lose sight of my companion, whose presence seem'd to stimulate me to equal exertions, I kept on my course notwithstanding the bad road which became worse as we proceeded.

After toiling along in this manner for an hour & a half, we suddenly came to the other extremity of the wood, where we found some of my foremost companions, many in a worse plight than myself.

Some had their feet already much blistered, others were obliged to change their shoes thus early in the day. After we had all assembled & refreshed ourselves with a little rest we again proceeded on our march. As to the chief who was to attend upon us, our baggage & eatables, they were left some distance behind.

About 11 o'clock being all exhausted, we made another halt, under a large tree, where we were determined to dine. Here we laid down & cooled ourselves, & by the time we were partially recovered from our fatigue, the remainder of our native party appeared with our refreshments. Our active purveyor Jos. Banks, was soon assiduously employed in getting our dinner ready. At about two, we again all started, tho feeling somewhat stiff & unwilling to proceed. At about four o'clock, we arrived at one of the sheds which Kahumanu had ordered to be erected for our convenience, & where she supposed we should pass the night.

The path we had hitherto followed, was still very rugged & painful to proceed upon, & many a groan issued from the possessors of worn out shoes, as they toiled limpingly along. The road which was

WAILUKU RIV[E]
"Transported down by the roaring torren[t]

R.D. del.t 1826.

a series of Lava rocks from the beginning to the end of our journey, was so very bad, & had so many inequalities & chasms continually in the way, that whilst walking you were unable to look at the surrounding scenery, without risking an immediate downfall. The sameness of the country however, through which we passed, possessed not sufficient allurements to draw us into this danger. After having left Yacaun [Waiakea] and the neighbourhood of Hido, with the exception of the wood I before mentioned, there are very few trees scattered over the face of the country. Lava rocks covered with long grass, or very large fern, with here and there a few straggling bushes, form the general appearance of the landscape.

As we had still several hours daylight before us, we were unwilling to lose the benefit of a fine afternoon, & determined therefore to push forward notwithstanding our prospect of bivouacking in the open air at night. Fortunately just before dark, when we had accomplished more than half our journey, we descried a couple of dismantled huts near the road side. Here, we determined to pass the night, & our attendants having arrived, we dispatched them around the country, to procure banana leaves, fern &c. to cover our huts for the night. Here we partook of a good supper, & then laid ourselves down comfortably to sleep.

With the morning's dawn we again prepared for our departure: as we had during the preceding day been gradually ascending the mountain, we now found the air uncommonly fresh & bracing, & therefore pursued our journey with great alacrity. We continued to ascend tho very gradually for the space of about 12 miles more, we were then informed that Paley would soon be in sight: shortly after we observed the smoke issuing from the crater, whose appearance we hailed with as much joy as the followers of Xenophon when the sea burst suddenly upon their sight. We hastened forward, though sometimes we were tempted from the path by the appearance of some very fine strawberries, which flourished in great abundance within a couple of miles of the volcano.

We now came to an abrupt declivity leading to a deep chasm which must formerly have been part of the volcano: trees and fern now plentifully cloathed its sides & bottom. Having descended, we again proceeded a few hundred yards, which brought us to the brink of a second precipitate descent also having marks of having anciently formed one of the boundaries of this immense volcano. The precipice from which we had a fine view of the crater itself, was difficult & dangerous to descend: on all sides were yawning chasms & vast apertures seemingly of very great depth. We now having pass'd a level space covered with cinders, arrived at the brink of this immense crater. The sight was most extraordinary & appalling, & amply repaid us for all our previous labour & fatigue.

The outward ridge of this formidable chaos of fiery smoke and lava, extends to the enormous distance of $7\frac{1}{2}$ miles in circumference: the Ledge itself is uniform & almost even all round & forms a precipitate cliff, abruptly descending to a shelving space from whence is a second cliff of narrower dimensions; the bottom of this forms the boundary of an immense plain of lava, assuming all shapes & colours. The descent from the brow of the highest ridge to the bottom of the crater we estimated to be about 2000 feet. Its situation & form were thus:

N
W
E
S
hut

On the surface of the volcanic plain below, were scattered an amazing number of small craters. About 20 of these were now in constant agitation: they were thrown up into pyramidal cones of from fifty to sixty feet high: from the top of each lava Pillar were ejected forth columns of dense smoke together with bursts of fire & lava, accompanied by a noise issuing simultaneously from each crater, similar to that attending the action of a blacksmiths bellows on a huge forge.

On the Southwest side of the Volcano appeared a very large crater, from which streams of red hot lava were continually pouring forth: the sight was most appalling, & the continual noise, as if all the Sicilian artificers were most busily engaged in their forging occupations, contributed greatly to give effect to the grandeur of the scene. On the East side of the Volcano, is a large hut built, which proved sufficiently extensive to accommodate our whole party. This hut had been erected for Kaopellani [Kapi'olani], a famous female chief, & the first Christian who ever descended into Paley.

ILAUEA CRATER
This formidable chaos of fiery smoke"

The largest of the cones, no later than five years ago, was revered as a God, & ceremoniously worshipped as such: offerings, such as Pigs, Bananas &c. were frequently left upon the first descent, to propitiate the favour of this igniferous Deity: the natives are yet extremely superstitious, & very few have the courage to venture into the abyss below, dreading the vengeance of the angry & deserted God.

When Kaopellani descended they say that it was universally expected that she would have been consumed: she undertook this toilsome journey & dangerous adventure, solely to prove the superiority of the religion she had just embraced, over that still upheld by her infatuated countrymen, & by her zeal, courage, & example, contributed greatly to the establishment of Christianity throughout the Sandwich Islands.

After dinner, some of our party determined to descend into these infernal regions. Three of them went down as far as the first ledge; there they met with so many difficulties in scrambling over chasms, beds of cinders, & loose lava stones, that they thought it prudent to reascend, satisfied with their evening's researches. As night came on the volcano appeared most magnificent. On all sides were the cones throwing up red hot cinders, & belching forth fire & smoke at a most furious rate. Around their bases flowed streams of burning lava which we now perceived were running [across?] the plain below in all directions. Having gratified our curiosity for some time in contemplating these wondrous Phenomena, we all retired to sleep. The Thermometer was as low as 54 deg., a change we felt most sensibly.

On the succeeding morning we arose by daybreak. I then prepared to make a drawing of this curious scene.

This employment kept me the whole morning, & in the mean time several of our party, headed by Lord Byron, made an attempt to explore the horrors of this Hell upon earth. They had nearly paid dear for their adventurous curiosity, as the wind when on their return suddenly shifting, the whole crater became involved in smoke. The Doctor assured me that, had this change of wind taken place a quarter of an hour sooner, when the party was advanced more into the bosom of the crater, their lives would have been in most imminent danger, from the malign influence of the sulphureous vapors, so thickly assailing them. As it was, they arrived at the hut completely exhausted. His Lordship gave me some account of his descent.

They experienced little difficulty in descending the first ledges; from thence they were obliged to walk almost to the opposite side of the Volcano, in order to assure to themselves the possibility of descending any lower. They were here met by our chaplain & naturalist, who gave them a most terrific account of the dangers they themselves had already experienced in their endeavours to descend, adding that it would be impossible to advance much farther without incurring imminent danger.

Notwithstanding, the exploring party still proceeded, & after experiencing most hair breadth escapes from their treading on faithless embers, & sinking neck deep into lava ashes, added to the sulphureous exhalations proceeding from the fissures they were constantly obliged to scramble over, they succeeded in reaching the lower ridges.

Here they were obliged to tread very circumspectly, making use of long sticks to prove the stability of this path. With great difficulty they arrived at the foot of one of the pillars I before mentioned: the noise, fire, & smoke proceeding from its cone, soon obliged them to retreat; they were much astonished at its magnitude. From the hut it only appeared to the eye, about twelve or fourteen feet high, instead of forty or fifty. I was unable to distinguish their figures at its base, without the aid of a telescope.

Their curiosity completely satiated, after having collected some specimens, they began ascending soon after the change of wind took place, & I think from the visiters' accounts, it would take some persuasion to induce them again to trust their persons in the abode of as fierce a God as Mr. Paley.

The fumes from the crater were so much felt even by us at the hut that we began to think seriously of decamping. Fortunately, to our great relief the wind in about half an hour, again shifted to its usual quarter. In the afternoon, our attendants having devoured their supplies of Poi &c., petitioned for a retrograde movement, & we therefore sent some of them off, & determined ourselves to leave so terrible a place early on the ensuing morning.

In the night our party were all awakened by the convulsive exertions of the pent up God. The earth upon which we slept trembled with the violence of his throes, & in a short time a new crater burst forth with a horrid noise immediately beneath our feet. Streams of burning lava flowed in every direction, accompanied with ejections of red hot ashes, & continual eructations of vast flames of fire. It was some time ere we could again compose ourselves to sleep.

On the ensuing morning we proceeded homeward. We left the crater at half past six, & arrived at the half way houses about one o'clock. Here we dined, supped, & slept, & early on the succeeding morning again continued our march. The jaunt back being down hill caused us much less fatigue: our feet also by this time were in some measure accustomed to the rugged nature of our lava path. By ten o'clock, we were again at the skirts of the direful wood, which however, we got thro pretty well, taking it leisurely & ever & anon refreshing exhausted nature with frequent libations of brandy & water. In the afternoon about three o'clock, we all congratulated each other upon our safely arriving at our house upon the point. Thus ended this most fatiguing but interesting journey: the pleasure of having visited by far the largest Volcano in the known world, completely banished from our minds all our past sufferings.

Having in the course of a day or two recovered from our fatigue, we began to think of leaving the harbour of Hido, or Yacaun, which from henceforth is to be denominated Byron's bay. Our purveyor Mr. Jos. Banks therefore set himself most actively to work, to procure us an ample supply of Pigs, Poultry, Yams &c., which were all sent on board as presents.

Kahumanu had also previously given orders for all the natives in the immediate district of Yacaun, to bring in the produce of their lands, as also a quantity of wood for fuel for the Frigate's consumption.

A day or two before we sailed, a great crowd of natives, to the number of three or four hundred, assembled round the old Queen's house bearing in their hands presents as tributes for her acceptance.

These people formed a singular & agreeable group. Some were laden with Tapa, others with wood, fruit & vegetables. Here & there one might perceive an unfortunate half starved Dog, destined as a gift to propitiate the favor of their mighty Queen.

Pigs, Poultry, Taro, Cocoanuts, and Yams arrived in great abundance, & were all duteously laid by the bearers at the feet of the old lady. She in her turn, with truly regal munificence, presented the whole to Lord Byron by which we were stocked with a sufficient quantity of these useful necessaries to load three or four boats.

We now once more prevailed upon our royal passengers to go on board & early on the 12th we bade adieu to Hido with the intention of returning to Woahoo, at which place we arrived on the succeeding evening, tho' too late to anchor.

We learnt next morning from the Kings pilot, an Englishman, that all our Honoruru friends were well: he however communicated to us other intelligence not of the most agreeable nature. During our absence an American vessel had arrived from the coast of California, having recently fallen in with the *Asia* Spanish 64 [guns], & two large brigs of war of the same nation, all which vessels were anchored at Monterry.

From the account given by the master of the American ship, it appeared that a mutiny had spread itself amongst these vessels. The crews had risen upon their officers, overpowered them, & after putting them all on shore together with Cantarac the Spanish General, & his followers, they proceeded to elect other officers, & had then commenced their piratical depredations. Our Yankee informant further assured us, that they had captured & burnt one American ship, & after having committed ravages on the coast, it was supposed that they would make for the Sandwich Islands, in order to recruit their stock of provisions.

This news as may well be imagined somewhat alarmed us; preparations were immediately made to put ourselves in a posture of defence; four of the Guns below, belonging to the captains cabin, were immediately mounted & all were loaded & double shotted.

Lord Byron now determined to contract his stay at Woahoo, which he resolved on leaving for good, in two days. The next morning I went on shore, to pick up if possible a cloak or tippet either by persuasion, or by offering my saddle in exchange, an article in great request amongst these islanders. I procured a beautiful tippet for my saddle, tho the chief with whom I bartered disgusted me not a little with his shuffling mode of dealing. Having by arrangement brought to him my bridle & saddle, I asked for his tippet. After considering for about two minutes, he suddenly exclaimed "me no like" & demanded Ten Dollars in addition. Determined not to be done by a Savage I indignantly snatched up my property, and was leaving his house, when he called me back, & after some little remonstrance we completed our original bargain. I also paid a parting visit to the queens. One of them presented me with a couple of mats. During these last two or three days, it was quite ridiculous to perceive us all actively employed in endeavouring to gain possession of cloaks, tippets, & other curiosities.

Each took on shore some little valuable, in order to effect a barter. Stationary of all kinds, broad cloth, ribbons &c., were all brought forth as objects of traffic. Ere we parted, about 12 cloaks, & twice as many tippets, had been thus given or purchased. Our surgeon, who had attended upon several of the chiefs, received many handsome presents. To Lord Byron also were given many Sandwich valuables. Indeed at the moment of our departure I think we spoiled the Sandwichers, as the Israelites of old treated the Egyptians.

On the 12th we bade our Honoruru friends a final adieu. Old Pitt, Boki and some of their attendants came on board. Karaimoku as well as Boki seemed very sorry to part with us. We weighed anchor & took our friends some little way out to sea.

The Regent appeared uncommonly well pleased with the frigate's fast sailing. He also requested to see the men at their quarters.

We now for the last time wished our friends good bye, & having sent them on shore we steered for Karakakooa [Kealakekua] to pick up our Surveyor Mr. Malden, as also to gratify our curiosity in the contemplation of the scene of Cook's calamitous death. Our useful attendant Sir Joseph Banks accompanied us. In two days we arrived off Karakakooa.

6

Adieu to the Sandwich Islands

This place affords an insecure & unpleasant anchorage. Owing to the very deep water, all vessels are obliged to anchor very near the shore, immediately below a lofty ridge of lava rocks, whose bases are washed by the sea. The village of Kayrooa [see note], where Cook was killed, forms one part of the bay; immediately opposite stands the village of Karakakooa, the bay being about a mile & a half wide: here was the Morai where Cook fixed his Observatory, the walls of which are still standing.

We were soon visited by Nahi [Nahe, Naihe], the chief person in the place; this man we had formerly known at Woahoo. He was the husband of the famous Kaopellani, & had rendered his name celebrated in the Sandwich school of eloquence; he was called their chief orator.

We were most kindly received by this distinguished couple, who appeared delighted to see their old acquaintance. They had an uncommon good house, situated within a few yards of the spot where Cook was killed.

Nahi was at that time a boy, & witnessed himself the death of this great circumnavigator. He took us to the spot, the rock on which Cook was standing when he received the fatal blow. King Tereoboo [Kalani'opu'u], whom Cook was endeavouring to persuade to come on board, was sitting on another rock within a few yards of him. On one side was a ledge of rocks upon which said Nahi the marines were drawn up. He also shewed us a cocoanut tree perforated by a ball from the *Discovery*'s launch.

According to his account, as long as Cook kept his face towards the natives they, respecting him as a God would not venture to attack his person. The man who wounded him first when in the act of desiring his men to cease firing was a common Kanaka, coming from a distant part of the island, & ignorant of Cook's attributed Divinity. Upon seeing him fall, several of the natives rushed forward, & immediately dispatched him with their clubs & war spears.

Nahi told us that when the firing first began, the people held up their war mats, finding these afforded them no shelter, they covered themselves with Tapa: they then dipped it in water, & lastly they held up their hands, thus vainly endeavouring to shelter themselves from the murderous effects of our firearms. He also says that about seventy

men fell in this fray, a far larger proportion than what is mentioned in Vancouver's voyages. We were then shown the Morai, which is now partially pulled down, where Cook's body was cut up & burned: many of the bones were carefully preserved, & considered by the natives as the most sacred relics. The burning of the body was an accustomed funeral rite paid to the highest deceased chiefs.

With the death of Cook, vanished the hostility of the islanders, & Nahi assured us that they regretted exceedingly what they had done. They even now look upon this event as a sort of national stigma upon their character & generally endeavour to evade all conversation relating to it.

On the next day the Governor John Adams or Coquini [Kuakini], came on board to breakfast. This man is about six feet four inches high, & weighs 28 stone [392 pounds], and is certainly in every sense of the word one of the greatest rogues that the island produces.

On the second morning after our arrival, a party was formed to visit a celebrated Morai, still existing in the neighbourhood, & the only building of the sort which has not been ransacked & despoiled. Indeed, so sacred has this Morai been held in the estimation of the natives, that no white man before our arrival had even by his presence profaned its threshold.

About a dozen of us accompanied John Adams & Nahi, who had been commanded by Karaimoku to allow Lord Byron & any he might choose to bring with him, free admittance to this pagan sanctuary.

After rowing round one of the points forming the bay of Karakakooa, the Morai suddenly opened upon our view: it was very prettily situated on the banks of a winding creek, & in the neighbourhood of a grove of cocoanut trees.

The exterior appearance of the building itself, was precisely like the large huts of the superior chiefs. This was encircled by a strong Palisadoe of trunks of cocoanut trees.

The fence formed a sort of court yard round the Morai. Here in all directions were planted rude looking carved wooden images, of all shapes & dimensions, whose misshapen forms & hideous countenances, exhibited a most grotesque spectacle. The Sandwich Gods, like most of the Deities revered by barbarous nations, are remarkable for their extreme ugliness & disproportions, the head being invariably four or five times as large as the rest of the body. Almost all the figures exhibited the same attitude; one however, I remarked tolerably well cut out, bearing a child in its arms. Added to these Deities were several long poles, on the tops of which were also carved small figures.

Immediately before the Morai outside of the Palisadoe, a solitary Deity presided, acting I suppose as a sort of centinel.

We now passed thro a low aperture into the interior. Here a spectacle extremely astonishing, presented itself to us.

On one side were arranged a great number of feathered Idols, protruding their misshapen heads thro' numberless folds of decayed Tapa.

Under these were deposited the bones of mighty kings & potent warriors, Sandwich heroes of other days, who once revered & worshipped these grim looking Idols as their Penates. Here were also carefully preserved the different weapons, used in warfare by these mighty chieftains, as also various articles of their dress, together with an infinite collection of antiquated rubbish, the superstitious offerings of these infatuated islanders.

An old Priest, the Guardian of these relics, still looked upon each of these grim looking Deities with the utmost veneration; when therefore it was made known to him that Lord Byron had procured Pitts consent to possess himself with the persons of as many Gods as he desired, the old mans indignation at this sacriligous rape became very apparent. He was obliged, however to submit. I had begun to sketch the inside of the Morai, having already finish'd one of its exterior appearance, when the rapacious inclinations of our party, suddenly began to manifest themselves. I threw aside my pencil, & regardless of the divine punishment attending such shameless sacrilege, took ample share in the depopulation of this ancient sanctuary.

Two frowning Gods, about twelve feet high, stood exactly opposite the door: at the feet of these the natives were accustomed to lay their offerings; these were quickly plucked up by the roots, & sent down as prizes to our boats.

I succeeded in appropriating to myself, a beautiful spear, (probably the mighty Pelian lance of a second Sandwich Achilles) a couple of

ᐊILUA BAY
ᐅbliged to anchor very near the shore"

KEALAKEKUA ▷
"Where Cook fixed his Observatory, the walls . . . are still standing"

Gods, & a few other curious articles within my reach, & as all the other visitants were equally piously inclined, nothing worth having remained, with the exception of the range of feathered Idols, to which were attached the royal bones. These, the old Priest determined to rescue from the general devastation, & resolutely refused to allow such sacred relics, to pass his threshold. Having thus gratified our curiosity, we returned on board, laden with the spoils of our heathen temple.

We remained at Karakakooa, four days, a space of time quite sufficient to explore everything of note, in its vicinity. As the scene of Capt. Cook's past exploits & death, it was a place to us all peculiarly interesting. To the memory of this zealous & ill fated officer Lord Byron determined to erect a sort of monument.

Having by chance a tolerable engraver on copper on board the following inscription

> SACRED TO THE MEMORY OF CAPT. JAS. COOK, R.N. (WHO DISCOVER'D THESE ISLANDS IN THE YEAR OF OUR LORD 1778, THIS HUMBLE MONUMENT IS ERECTED BY HIS COUNTRYMEN IN THE YEAR OF OUR LORD 1825.)

was cut out upon a piece of this metal, which being firmly let into a block of wood about ten inches long was affixed to another piece forming a cross about ten feet high. This monument, the only thing of the kind within range of our ability to execute during our short stay, was placed on a hill in the centre of the ruins of the Morai, the spot upon which Cook's body was cut up & burned. It may distinctly be seen by vessels when entering the harbour.

It appears astonishing that Cook should have remained so long in the harbour of Karakakooa, without attempting to explore the neighbouring islands in search of a better anchorage.

Its appearance is most sterile & uninviting & water is not to be procured except by sending five miles into the interior for it: added to this, such vast chains of lava are dispersed thro' the district that ground for cultivation is so scarce, as frequently to produce severe famine in the neighbourhood.

I saw very few good looking natives. Our treatment from Nahi, was more cordial than any thing we had previously met with. He loaded us with curiosities, provisions we had no need of, & seemed much concerned when the moment of departure arrived. The unwieldy pudding headed John Adams, was the exact reverse: on the morning of our departure, he actually came on board, bringing tippets, & other curiosities, for which he demanded a most exorbitant price.

We felt so indignant at his mercenary views, (accustomed so long to receive Gratis, from the hands of these people,) that we soon handed our fat friend over the side, somewhat to his mortification and disappointment.

At midnight on Sunday, the 18th we bade adieu to the Sandwich Islands, & our determination was then to proceed direct to the Society Isles. We had originally supposed that our stay with our Sandwich friends, would have been of much greater duration: fortunately, circumstances were so happily combined, as to reduce this time to a month less than we had expected.

We arrived amongst these tawny islanders at a most auspicious moment: by our weight & remonstrances, we thoroughly succeeded in establishing, & strengthening the young King on his throne. Pitt was restored to good health, & the nation, by the skill of our Surgeon, & Lord Byron by his condescencion & proper management acquired the entire goodwill & friendship of the natives, who on all occasions were exceedingly accommodating, & loaded our ship with supplies of every description. Mr. Malden, soon accomplished his task in the surveying department, which was another motive for abridging our stay.

Certainly no ship will hereafter visit these Islands, under such advantageous circumstances as the *Blonde*, & in taking a retrospective view of their attentions to us during our stay amongst them, I think as a nation they have exceeded in gratitude, goodwill, & liberality, our most sanguine expectations.

◁ KA'AWALOA
"The rock on which Cook . . . received the fatal blow"

HALE O KEAV
"A celebrated Mora

R.D. delt. 1826.

R.D. delt 1826.

7
Islands in the Pacific

Our usual good luck in continually effecting such happy passages, completely deserted us on our voyage to Otaheite [Tahiti], after buoying up our spirits, with the first ten days of excellent run. Suddenly we encounter'd baffling & contrary winds, which began, by their obstinate adherence to the same quarter, to preclude all hopes of our reaching the desired Port.

We were however in some measure reconciled to this disappointment, from our being destined to make further discoveries in this vast expanse of sea.

Early on the morning of the 30th, an island was descried from the mast head. Altho differing in point of latitude five degrees, we supposed this to be Starbucks island, which had been discovered in a whaler by a master of this name, some time ago, on his return home [to London] with the royal Sandwichers on board.

About noon, we hove to abreast of this island, which appeared to be a narrow strip of low coral beach, extending to the distance of eight or ten miles, & exhibiting little vegetation with the exception of a few clumps of thick freak [?] looking trees; these were so compact in form, that at some distance they resembled rocks, & until our nearer approach, were taken for such.

Mr. Malden was dispatched on shore to survey this unknown region more accurately: the cutter also took some of our officers. I unfortunately was not of the party, as I had hoped another opportunity would have offered itself in the afternoon. The party was enabled to land with safety, notwithstanding they were accompanied to the beach, which was shelving & precipitous by a large number of Sharks which were so ravenous, and hostilely inclined, that they actually seized on the blades of the oars, as they were dipped into the water.

They found the island to be composed of one entire bed of coral. Shells of all descriptions were everywhere scattered about: some very curious specimens were brought on board.

Large families of sea birds occupied this dreary, seagirt spot; these were so tame, as to allow themselves to be taken from their nests, or knocked on the head with sticks: there were some beautiful Tropic birds amongst them.

MALDEN ISLAND, PACIFIC
"Squares, composed of walls of coral rock"

Vegetation was only to be observed in thin and scattered patches: the genus of the trees I before mentioned, was totally unknown to our Botanist.

No vestiges of habitations were found, altho' several squares, composed of walls of coral rock, in height about three feet, were observed in many places: in the midst of each square was placed a pile of coral stones, resembling a rude sort of altar.

These seemed to indicate that this place had been visited by some of the neighbouring nations. It is rather singular, that Cook likewise mentions having remarked the same sort of regular edifice, which cannot be the work of chance, in one of the islands amongst his discoveries.

In the afternoon the whole party returned to the ship, & we again made sail, tho' not without some degree of uneasiness at the idea of bumping in a dark night upon one of these unknown coral shores. This discovery was called Malden's island in compliment to our Surveyor.

Another day or two's sail proved to us that Capt. Starbuck had made no error in the position of his island: we made it on the morning of the 1st August. Its appearance was even more wretched & uninviting then Malden's island; not a vestige of verdure of any kind was to be seen upon it.

Our wind still proved adverse for Otaheite. On the 9th to our great surprise, land was again seen from the mast head, which upon our nearer approach, we supposed to be Watteoo [Atiu, Hervey Islands], a small inhabited island mentioned in Cook's voyages, as existing near the spot. We did not however feel at all assured in this opinion, as the latitude laid down by Cook, differed many miles from that of the island now before us.

In the afternoon, we were within a few miles of the nearest point. A heavy swell rolled towards the land, which caused a tremendous surf upon a chain of coral, which appeared to encircle the island: beyond this it seemed thickly wooded.

We in vain endeavoured to descry any sign of its being inhabited: no canoes were visible, nor could we perceive with our glasses, any signs of habitations.

On a sudden, to our great joy, we beheld a native emerging from the wood; he fixed himself upon a rock, & remained for some time attentively watching the ship.

A boat was immediately lowered, & Mr. Malden, attended by a couple of marines armed, was deputed to approach the shore, & endeavour to ascertain something respecting its inhabitants tho he was ordered not to land.

As he advanced, we perceived the native retire into the woods, where he remained concealed for some time. He at last ventured from his hiding place, but could not be prevailed upon to swim off to the boat, but by continued gesticulations, he seemed to point out that a better landing place might be procured on the other side of the island. Mr. Malden returned on board, & told us, that during his parley with the man we had observed, he could distinctly perceive several tawny visages continually protruding themselves thro' the leafy covert overhanging the rocks.

Upon receiving this intelligence the Captain determined to stand off & on during the night, and on the following morning, if possible, by getting one of the natives on board, he hoped to procure some information respecting the land before us. On the succeeding morning, we proceeded round a point, in order to get at the lee side, where we hoped to meet with some canoes.

Shortly after breakfast, we perceived two or three canoes making towards us. We consequently lay to at about six miles distance from the land.

One of the canoes in which was a single man, soon came alongside, & with very little persuasion, a rope having been handed to him, leapt on board. The costume of our visitor & of those in the other canoes approaching, soon put to flight our hopes of being the first discoverers, as likewise our fears of having our persons converted into steaks for the feasts of cannibals.

Our friend had on a straw hat made precisely after the European form; he was clothed in a garment of Tapa, which however was differently worn from those at the Sandwich Islands.

The one he had on was a complete Spanish Poncho, being a square thick piece of Tapa, curiously painted, in the midst of which was an opening cut for the entrance of the head, the garment flowing down behind & before, precisely like the South American Ponchos.

Whilst questioning our visitor, who spoke a language very much resembling the Sandwich tongue, another canoe came along side.

The appearance of this canoe was quite novel to us. Unlike those of the Sandwich isles, altho double, it was formed towards the stern into one canoe. This stern, curiously carved, was carried up in an inward circular direction to about seven feet from the water. In this manner I believe are formed all the Society Island canoes.

Two persons, who by their dress and appearance bespoke them to be of some importance now stepped on board; they both to our wondering eyes exhibited a couple of letters which had been given them by a member of the London missionary society, at Otaheite, & which qualified them to act as native teachers, at this island, which they called Mauti [Mauke, Cook Islands].

The dress of these visitors, who were particularly fine made athletic young men, consisted of cotton shirts, blue cloth waistcoats, & very fine mats passed round their waists to supply the deficiency of trowsers, a costume savouring of some earlier visitation than our own to this island. We however felt puzzled, as it was very evident that this could not be Watteoo, the island we originally supposed it was, for on being questioned respecting that island they immediately nodded their heads, intimating by signs, that it existed at some distance off.

They were then invited into the Captain's cabin, & by their astonishment clearly proved that at all events, they had never before seen a ship of our size & dimensions.

Bread, & wine, & water were offered to them: they repeatedly smelt the former, before they ventured to taste it, & upon sipping some of the wine, their wry faces soon explained to us that it was not exactly to the gusto of their barbarous palates.

I was much amused at the astonishment & curiosity excited in these poor fellows, & took them round the ship to increase their surprize. The sight of our galley fire, and the dinner getting ready, were objects of amazing interest, as also the great guns, with whose destructive powers, they seemed perfectly acquainted. I took them where the Band was standing playing: the brazen instruments, & inflated cheeks of the performers added greatly to their surprize and amusement.

It is very remarkable that Music had no charms for a Sandwich ear: in the presence of our band when performing, they evinced the utmost apathy & indifference. The conduct of these men formed a great contrast, which was observed by us all. As these missionaries repeatedly assured us that we might land in safety, Lord Byron determined to go on shore: he kindly offered to give me a passage in his boat; he also took one of the missionaries with him, in order that he might show us the most convenient landing place.

The other followed with some of our officers in the cutter. Upon approaching the shore & being shewn the landing place, where were assembled a great number of natives, we began to be rather apprehensive for the safety of our boat, as a tremendous surf was then dashing upon the coral bank, upon which we were to effect our disembarkation.

After some consideration, it was determined that we should remove into a large canoe which the natives had launched for our convenience.

By seizing on the moment when the waves were precipitated with less violence on the beach, we were landed in perfect safety. Boats attempting to land here, & the sailors unacquainted with the propitious moment would inevitably be dashed to pieces. The Cutters crew followed our example. The coral bank which is constantly overflowed, stretches about fifty yards distant from the shore, we were therefore all carried on the backs of the islanders to a dry spot.

We were here greeted by a large assembly of wondering natives, who were very forward in their demonstrations of joy, each individual not feeling himself happy except by being honoured with a hearty shake by the hand.

Amongst the rest were two women, the wives of our friends the missionaries.

We were much surprised to observe that they had on large poke bonnets, made precisely after the English fashion: the remainder of their dress consisted of white tapa.

Unlike the Sandwich women who amongst the lower orders, invariably expose the shoulders & bosom, all the females we here saw were not so prodigal in displaying their native charms of their persons: on the contrary they universally appeared, muffled closely, wearing an upper garment of tapa, in the same manner that an English lady would wear her shawl.

This friendly greeting now having taken place, we were led thro' a thick shady wood, supposing shortly to arrive at the huts of some of the inhabitants. At a large open space at the commencement of the wood, a very handsome canoe was building: it was chiseled out with very great care, & about 80 feet long, being thus rendered capable of visiting the neighbouring islands.

Its form was precisely that of the one I before mentioned.

The first part of our walk was none of the pleasantest, the path which reached about a mile, being composed of sharp pointed coral stones: on a sudden we came upon the verge of a most beautiful lawn: the path, now no longer of coral, winded thro a grove of very fine trees, (one I measured 20 feet in circumference about the trunk). At each moment the surrounding scenery became more beautiful.

We now arrived at an open space where were built two of the prettiest, & most romantically situated cottages imaginable: these proved to be the dwellings of the missionaries themselves, who were in fact the chief personages of the island.

Our surprise was great indeed in beholding the neatness & regularity of these buildings, & we now felt more assured than ever, that we were not the first white people that these islanders had yet beheld. The houses looked like neat English cottages: the outside walls were whitewashed, & the roofs thatched with long grass. Around each dwelling was a strong Palisadoe; the enclosure formed a sort of garden. The inside of these houses corresponded with their exterior neatness: the principal room was boarded; a sofa & chairs evidently made by the natives were the household furniture. Windows with shutters, something like our Venetian blinds, added to the coolness & comfort of the apartment.

We were also struck with the neatness of the bedrooms, which were parted off with skreens of Tapa; in these were beds, their furniture also of tapa. An oilcloth carpet of the same material completed their comfortable & civilized appearance, & when contrasting the vile filthy huts of the Sandwichers, with the elegant simplicity universally perceptible here, how very low did the former sink in our estimation.

The conduct of these people was infinitely more chaste & decorous than that of our former friends: here indeed the women seemed to entertain a high sense of modesty, which at the Sandwich Islands, I am concerned to say, is totally laid aside by both sexes.

The primitive simplicity of these people called forcibly to my mind, the fabled times of the Golden age.

Our kind hosts now treated us with a native feast, consisting of baked Pig, fried Breadfruit & Yams, Poi they had none, after which one of the missionaries took us to see their church, which again excited our surprize and admiration.

This building was beautifully situated on a rising ground, upon the lawn I before mentioned. There was a Palisadoe fence of stumps of cocoanut trees, around it: through this fence, two neat paths also edged with stumps of trees, led you to the two doors of the church, which was an oval building having about twenty windows, & sufficiently large to accommodate with ease, a congregation of three hundred people. In the centre, near the wall, was a pulpit, precisely in form like that of an English country church. Its shape was octagon, & the entrance was at the part nearest the wall: it was elevated about twenty feet from the ground, from which was a regular flight of steps, for the convenience of the preacher. Immediately below was the reading desk. On all sides were long benches to accommodate the congregation. Both pulpit and reading desk were painted black, on which were drawn in red & yellow paint, ornamented designs & borders.

Here indeed was amply shewn, the progress in civilization, to which this interesting little community had already arrived. We had seen nothing of the kind at the Sandwich Islands: their places of worship were exactly like the wretched huts in which they dwell.

The population of this island, amounted to about three hundred souls. In the afternoon, we returned again to the seashore, having bartered with great success amongst the natives. I procured a beautiful spear & one or two other curiosities. Scissors & knives were held by them, in the highest estimation: they seemed perfectly acquainted with their utility. I observed one man having exchanged something for an anchor button, running off, and shewing by his gestures as if he had completely duped the person with whom he had been dealing. Our naturalist shot several rare and beautiful birds: unfortunately our botanist was not on shore: he would no doubt have found much to

MAUKE, COOK ISLAN
"The dwellings of the missionarie

interest him in the vegetable productions of the island. We took to him on board several curious specimens, which he had never before met with.

We now all collected our different purchases and prepared for our departure on board. The surf had increased greatly since our landing, & our embarkation appeared fraught with danger: any mismanagement on the part of our native conductors would have exposed us to the greatest risk. Fortunately we got off to our boats in perfect safety, & having arrived on board about six o'clock made sail, & bade adieu to the hospitable regions of Mauti which we now denominated Parry's island.

We were all very anxious to find out what ship had previously visited this island, as the natives were too well acquainted with articles of European manufacture, to allow us to suppose that we were the first discoverers. Our anxiety & doubt were soon cleared up: upon referring to the latest reports printed by the missionary society, we found that this island comprises one of the group called Harvey's [Hervey] islands: it is not however noticed in any of the charts which we have on board.

Mr. Williams & Mr. Bourne, belonging to the missionary society at Otaheite, accompanied by two native Teachers, visited it in 1824 in the Brig *Endeavour*, a vessel belonging to the Chiefs of the Leeward Islands.

They had previously touched at Atui, also composing one of the Harveys group, the authority of whose King was acknowledged by the people of Mauti.

Having persuaded him to embrace the Christian religion they also prevailed upon him to accompany them to the other islands obedient to his sway, & finally, by their arguments, & the King's authority, the Xtian religion was established throughout the whole group, & native teachers sent to all of them.

Our ship was the second only that these people had seen on their coast.

Our wind continued contrary until the 1st of September, when it suddenly became fair for the coast; we therefore gave up all hopes of seeing Otaheite, & forthwith made the best of our way for Valparaiso.

After this period we were constantly blest with such favoring breezes, that during twenty one days, we averaged something more than 197½ miles per day, thus running over above 4000 miles in the short space of three weeks: this passage may be considered wonderful. Certainly no ship has perhaps taken so long a cruize as the *Blonde*, at the same time enjoying such a series of uninterrupted fine weather.

8

Chile: Valparaíso to Concepción

On Sunday afternoon, still carrying with us our favoring breezes, we made the Island of Juan Fernandez. The bold rocky outline of its mountains which appear very high, has a fine effect from the sea; the vallies, & low land, seemed uncommonly rich & verdant. Calling to mind the beautiful tale of Robinson Crusoe, one gazed on this island with peculiar interest. Goats, which I believe thrive there in great abundance, are now its sole proprietors. Formerly convicts from the Chilian states were banished to this desolate spot.

Eight months had now elapsed, during which period, we had been entirely deprived of all civilized communication; we were completely ignorant of the political state of affairs in our own country, and as the rumour of a probability of a war with France, had existed upon our last leaving South America, we again approached its coast with feelings of great anxiety & impatience.

On the afternoon of the 22d September, we once more hailed the appearance of a civilized Christian like country. A fine stiff breeze prevailing, & our gallant Frigate going thro' the water at the rate of 12 Knots per hour, soon brought us near Angel Point, off which the ship lay to, & Lord Byron, myself, & Mr. Malden, proceeded on shore in the Gig. Upon landing, we were delighted to find that our expectation of a war, was quite unfounded.

Our sudden reappearance, (no one being apprised of the *Blonde*'s arrival,) quite startled the family of the British Consul, who could hardly be persuaded that we had already accomplished our mission to the Sandwich Islands. We were soon put in possession of our letters: a large collection had been awaiting our arrival at Valparaiso. We here found at anchor in the harbour, the *Cambridge*, *Briton*, *Mersey*, & *Tartar*, the latter preparing in a few days to leave this place for England.

On the succeeding morning I was agreeably surprised to observe how much the winter season had improved the appearance of Valparaiso.

The hills overhanging the town, which we had left clothed in a homely garb of sober russet, were now dressed out in lively green, their sides interspersed with beautiful creepers, & wild flowers, of which there are a vast variety here during the rainy months.

The temperature of the air was also delightful, the strong, gusty, southern breezes, having given place to winds less violent, & which altho more cold & bracing were infinitely more pleasant.

Capt. Maling had long been intending to take a trip to Conception, both for the purpose of procuring wood & coals, (which necessary articles are found there in great abundance[)] & also of seeing that part of the country of South America, which is reckoned the most fertile, & beautiful spot of the whole of the Chilian territories. The *Blonde* being also sadly deficient in Coals, fuel, & water, Lord Byron was tempted to accompany Capt. Maling, who also persuaded Sir Murray Maxwell of the *Briton*, with his Frigate to be of the party.

Ere this plan was put in execution, a fortnight passed away at Valparaiso. By the way of amusing ourselves & friends here, a play was started amongst the officers of the different ships, to be performed on shore, where we hired a commodious room, & the first Lieutenant of the *Cambridge* & myself, busied ourselves unremittingly for a couple of days in painting scenes for the occasion.

The representation of "She stoops to conquer" went off with great eclat to a crowded assembly, who pronounced it inimitable. Fortunately we had a most excellent Tony Lumkin [Lumpkin], whose original exertions enhanced exceedingly the value of the performance.

Some of our officers also, in conjunction with two or three others of the *Tartar*, & *Mersey*, gave a ball and supper to an elegant assemblage of fair belles of Valparaiso. The united bands of the *Cambridge*, & *Blonde*, attended, & the evening passed merrily away, redounding much to the credit of the liberal supporters of the entertainment.

Thus we amused ourselves until the 22d, upon which day a signal was made for the whole squadron to weigh anchor.

It was a beautiful morning: & the sight of four English men of war, leaving the harbour at the same moment, was sufficiently attractive to draw to the neighbouring hills, many of our acquaintance to witness their departure. The British consul Mr. Nugent having some business with the government at Conception, took a passage with Capt. Maling in the *Cambridge*.

The *Mersey* was destined to proceed to Coquimbo. Notwithstanding the *Blonde* had traversed so vast an expanse of ocean, continually effecting such happy passages, still our invidious friends in the accompanying ships, had presumptuously decided that she was no sailer. Owing to her appearance, being light, & carrying her Guns very high from the water, added to her capability of stowing an immense stock of provisions & water, she had been opprobriously designated the Tea chest.

Our opponents were very sanguine: the *Briton* being considered a notorious clipper, & the *Cambridge* having given the go by to every vessel she had hitherto sailed with. Our passage to Conception, which port lies about two hundred miles to the Southward of Valparaiso, being a dead beat to windward, was performed in eight days, & I am happy to add that our adversaries were completely deceived in their expectations of beating us.

When light winds prevailed, we decidedly had the advantage, & could triumphantly spare them both several sails, & during a heavy breeze, we speedily passed the *Cambridge* & gallantly maintained our own, (as sailors have it) even with our far famed expeditious opponent the *Briton*.

After this contest, our reputation, as being a very tolerable sailer, was fully established.

On the 30th we entered the harbour of Talcuhana [Talcahuano], this being the sea port of the city of Conception. It deservedly merits being reckoned one of the best ports on this side of South America. The entrance is much protected by the small island of Queriquina, & the bay which is exceedingly capacious is partially shut out from the violent winds, frequently prevailing in the winter months, from the North, & which sometimes renders the anchorage at Valparaiso exceedingly dangerous & insecure. On either side as we entered this magnificent port, the delighted eye reposed on lofty hills, their summits down to the waters edge, thickly clothed, with beautiful woodland scenery.

The anchorage which is immediately opposite the village of Talcuhana, is reckoned about twelve or thirteen miles from the entrance into the bay.

The village itself, is an inconsiderable dirty place, being simply a collection of fishermen's cottages, an insignificant fortress, & a range

BAY OF CONCEPCIÓN, CHIL
"This magnificent port

R.D. del^t 1826.

of warehouses, built for the reception of goods intended for the Conception market.

The arm of land, upon which this village is situated, & which forms a part of the bay, surpasses in richness, variety of scenery, and luxuriance of vegetation anything I have hitherto beheld on this side of Cape Horn. It has precisely the appearance of a Gentlemans Park, in a high state of cultivation. Fine verdant lawns, thickly interspersed with beautiful trees of various shades, which here & there form natural enclosures, characterize the scenery: amongst these are fields of barley & wheat, apparently in a most thriving state. A day or two after our arrival, a message was dispatched to the Intendente, or Governor of this province, intimating the Captains, & British Consul's desire of paying him a visit.

They were invited to the city on the 19th, which was a grand feast day, & the Intendente obligingly sent to the port, several of his horses for the accommodation of his visiters.

Great preparations had been made for their reception. I was anxious to see the city, & inhabitants to the greatest advantage, & therefore obtained permission from Capt. Maling, to make one of the party.

We formed rather an imposing cavalcade: the party consisted of the three Captains in their full dress, Mr. Nugent & his Vice consul, also in their uniforms, & myself, with two other Gentlemen as interpreters.

The town is at the distance of about eight or nine miles from the sea port: the hills which surround it, prevent its being seen from the anchorages. A soldier had been ordered to be our conductor to it.

The road for the first four miles is over an extensive plain, some parts of which being very swampy, render an experienced guide extremely useful.

The remainder of the ride is very beautiful, the country surrounding you being thickly wooded, & presenting continually very picturesque views.

The town of Conception suddenly opens upon you when within about a mile of its suburbs. It appears advantageously situated on a plain partially surrounded by lofty hills. The majestic river BioBio, the boundary of the Araucanian territories, flows past the town within about 2 miles. From the high land at Talcuhana, its course can plainly be traced, winding for many leagues into the interior, until shut from your view by the distant mountains.

As we arrived at the skirts of the town, we were surprised to observe several pieces of artillery drawn out, & as we approached, a salute of 21 Guns, was fired in honour of our arrival.

Our guide conducted us thro' several streets whose desolate appearance, told a melancholy tale of the ravages committed in the late contests with the Spaniards, & the state's more inveterate enemies the Indians.

Altho' owing to the novelty of the arrival of such distinguished guests, added to its being a feast day, the streets were thronged with well dressed curious Spectators, still the complete air of desolation which pervades this devoted town, struck us as strangers, most forcibly.

Grass is allowed to grow abundantly in the streets, which as at SantIago, are all built at right angles: the houses are likewise mostly on ground floors. Above one half of the town is in an utter state of ruin: on all sides are tottering walls, & mouldering edifices, their sides thickly shrouded with long grass, & twining creepers: some were entirely laid prostrate, & again successive vacant spaces pointed out that here the unsparing hand of war had been more particularly active.

In many parts fences alone proclaimed the former existence of buildings; even the churches had not escaped the general devastation: their drooping spires, and dismantled towers proclaimed from afar the miserable state of this town, which has been taken and pillaged by prevailing parties, no less than six successive times.

We were conducted thro' several streets, until we arrived at the Plaza, or square, where a body of troops was drawn up to receive us: they presented arms as we passed.

The palace occupied one side of the square: here we alighted & were received with every mark of respect by the Intendente & his

Staff, all equipped in Gala uniform. We were led into a large Sala, & presently introduced to our hosts wife, whom I thought the prettiest woman I had yet seen in Chili.

Until dinner time, we sauntered about the town, & I was glad to observe that the inhabitants recovering from the disasters of the late wars, are beginning to repair their dilapidated houses.

I saw many new unfinished buildings. The place seems to possess a very limited population; they have conceived that a colony from England is about to come out & settle in their territories.

I was repeatedly asked if this was not the intention of a party of our countrymen, to whom they appear uncommonly well inclined.

On our return to the palace, we found that amongst other visiters to compliment us upon our arrival were the two famous Araucanian chiefs Venancio & Peneleo: the former appears a hearty chuckling old blade, & I soon became his most intimate friend, whilst the latter of whom Capt. Hall gives so delightful a character, is distant & reserved, & his scowling brow & sullen looks, plainly indicated the natural ferocity of his disposition.

These chiefs are in the pay of the Chilian Government, who find it political to make friends with their dangerous and restless neighbors the Araucanians, over whom Venancio, and his chieftain brother possess unbounded authority.

Dinner being announced, we all adjourned to the *Sala de comer*: this was the first time I had ever partaken of a Chilian banquet. The different dishes with the exception of a few savouring too strongly of oil & fatness, were tolerably well cooked; the unpleasant part of the entertainment however was the immense number of courses, which followed each other in quick succession, & of which the already satiated guest could not refuse partaking, without infringing on the rules of Chilian politesse.

Ten courses, consisting of every imaginable dainty, in the form of fish, fowl, & flesh, thus in turn loaded the groaning board. I was seated next to my Indian friend Venancio, & was amused to observe his ready dispatch & entire devotion, towards disencumbering the Intendente's table of its numerous superfluities. He was equally liberal & attentive in his Bacchanalian exertions, & having emptied his own decanter very soon applied to the bounty of his nearest neighbours.

During the entertainment, appropriate toasts were drunk by both parties, & a band of musicians stationed in the antichamber "fill'd each pause" a lack of talk "had made" by giving vent to a collection of brazen instruments, almost too powerful for our auricular nerves.

Our hospitable entertainer had intended to have finished the day's convivialities with a ball. Capt. Maling however was obliged to return early on board; this part of the entertainment was consequently deferred.

Towards evening we wished our friends adieu, promising at their repeated sollicitations, to return in a few days, & make them a longer visit.

On the 4th October, H.M.[S.] *Tartar*, arrived from Valparaiso, touching here in her passage to England. As we had now a very strong force of marines, the different companies of the various ships amounting to about three hundred men, it was determined that the 7th should be a grand review day.

Notice was therefore dispatched to the Governor, who promised to be present with a party of his friends. He also in his turn assured us of a military treat, as Venancio, & Peneleo, were to attend, bringing with them a band of Indians, who appropriately accoutered, were also to go thro' their warlike evolutions.

The rumour of this spectacle, caused a great bustle in the city, & surrounding neighbourhood, & on the preceding day, many *Carritas* were constantly arriving at the port, preciously laden with numberless fair spectators for the approaching novel scene.

On the 11th, a fine cloudless day, the Intendente & his friends, & various large parties were early assembled on the appointed spot, which was a level space upon the hills above the village of Talcuhana.

The troops were all disembarked about ten o'clock. Venancio, Peneleo, & their band of Araucanians, soon made their appearance. They were in number about two hundred, & as they approached in an irregular manner they continually brandished long lances with which they were all furnished, uttering at the same time their discordant piercing warhoop. They were all mounted on horseback, & variously accoutered. I never beheld such a troop of singular wild looking creatures: they possessed countenances I think fully indicative of the restless ferocity of their character.

Some of these were but partially clothed, having nothing more than short trowsers made of the skins of animals, or a piece of coarse cloth round their middle.

All possessed Ponchas, which with their *Lazas* formed a part of their saddle furniture: few of them had any covering for their heads, but allowed their long shaggy black hair to float in dark masses around their faces, thus heightening the natural ferocity of their features.

All had long iron spurs affixed to their naked heels. They are not at all a muscular athletic race of men; their necks are particularly short, & thick, and their shoulders, high and stooping, give them a very awkward appearance.

Their horses partake much of the wild & barbarous air of their masters, being mostly a herd of lank, rawboned wretched looking animals.

Many of the troop possessed swords, which they seemed to wield with great dexterity; all had likewise an enormous long lance.

By the command of Venancio, they went thro' their exercise. On a signal given, they all scampered off in a body, brandishing their spears & ringing their warhoop: they would then precipitately retreat, & draw up in a body, their commanders repeatedly galloping round the little troop, all simultaneously hooting & shouting most discordantly.

Again, they would quickly dismount, & advance to the charge, using the most extraordinary gestures, leaping forward, beating their long lances against the ground & by loud cries & howlings apparently endeavouring to work each other up to a fitting frenzy, for advancing with all due hostility to the attack.

In return for this display, our Troops went thro' their manoeuvres, which seemed to afford all parties the highest entertainment.

I think I have seldom witnessed a spectacle more highly pleasing & picturesque. The review ground was one of those beautiful natural

lawns I before described, upon the verge of a very high hill: the surrounding scenery exhibited the most extraordinary richness, trees of every hue of green, and brilliant copse-wood thickly clothing the immediate neighbourhood. Below your feet, were the village of Talcuhana, & the ships of war, calmly reposing at anchor in the bay: the extreme distance was bounded by a chain of lofty mountains, & the hills surrounding the city of Conception, whilst the great BioBio, in a vast azure sheet, winded majestically around their bases.

The foreground of this comprehensive picture, was singularly striking & animated.

On one side were drawn up our British troops, in compact martial array. Fronting them were our wild friends the Araucanians, whose singular air, savage appearance, & original accoutrements contrasted finely with the beautiful regular lines which our Marines displayed: the mid-space was graced with the presence of gaily dressed ladies['] military & naval beaus, together with the Peasantry of the country with their handsomely striped, parti-coloured Ponchas.

At the end of the week, our party paid a second visit to Conception, intending to honour our friends with two or three days of our company. The Intendente provided beds for one half of his visiters, & the remainder were lodged with an English resident of the place.

Our promised ball took place on the first evening of our arrival. Conception is renowned for pretty women. I must own, I was sadly disappointed in the paucity of beauty observable in the fair part of the creation which graced the entertainment. Scarcely a pretty face was to be seen; the ladies were also dressed abominably ill, few even wearing those necessary accompaniments towards the perfection of a good figure, a pair of Stays. I was astonished to observe chairs & benches placed in the antichamber leading to the ballroom, where were sitting a vast number of females, wrapt up in shawls, having only a small part of their faces visible. They were eagerly intent upon what was going forward in the ballroom; I found upon enquiry that the most respectable families thus frequent entertainments, & remain shrowded in a large shawl, incog for the evening: these visiters are called Tapadas, & no ball can take place without having the doors, windows & antichambers, crowded with them.

Spanish country dances, reels & minuets, were footed in quick succession; the latter is a particularly favourite dance in Chili, & is mostly patronized by fat elderly ladies, who having lost the springiness & vivacity of youth, become performers in these sober dances, and with half averted face, & profound genuflexions they sidle about the room, causing the most ludicrous exhibition imaginable.

The next morning I sallied forth, in order to see something more of the town. A neighbouring hill, where is built a fortress, called the battery of Benevideo (that pirate having formerly erected it in order to annoy the city,) commands a very beautiful, & extensive view. The whole town is stretched at your feet, & in the distance you can distinctly descry the entrance into the harbour, & the ships laying at anchor in the bay of Talcuhana.

I was also taken by Peneleo to the quarters allotted for the Indians, which are in the suburbs.

I intended paying a visit to my friend Venancio, he having promised to sit for his picture. The old chief was enjoying a sound sleep, from which my conductor deemed it not advisable to arouse him. I therefore passed on to see Peneleo's family. I presently entered a low narrow hut, and was soon introduced to his relations. They came flocking around me about fifteen in number, mostly women & children. There were two young Indian females remarkably pretty; they had fine laughing dark eyes, good mouths, & regular white teeth; a fresh rubicund colour beamed forth beneath their tawny transparent complexions. Their dress was neatly becoming, their long black hair was partly braided, (interwoven with brads) around their foreheads, whilst a few plaited tresses depended behind: to the ends of these were whimsically fastened several brazen thimbles. A piece of coarse worsted cloth was hung round their shoulders, fastened before by an immensely long silver pin, the top of which was flat & about three inches in diameter. Another piece of cloth, fastened round their waists by a very broad, gaily striped band of worsted completed their becoming decorations.

They seemed very curious, examining every part of my dress, with great attention, & frequently burying their hands in my pockets, which manoeuvre considering as a hint, I distributed amongst them several quarter Dollars, this put them in the highest good humour. I endeavoured to make a sketch of an old woman who had two immense silver ornaments of this shape pendent from her ears. She however, as well as the younger part of the community, could not be prevailed upon to remain stationary. Peneleo himself seemed to do the honours of his house with suspicious reluctance. I therefore very shortly took my leave of him. Having spent two days with our friends at Conception, we again returned to the port, & a day or two before our departure, Captn. Maling invited the Governor & suite on board, & treated them with a handsome entertainment.

9
Return to Valparaíso

On the 9th the *Tartar* left us, sailing direct for Rio de Janeiro, & on the 12th the squadron again weighed anchor, in order to return to Valparaiso. The *Cambridge* & *Briton*, fearful of granting us another triumph, (it being clearly understood that the *Blonde* sails best, when going perfectly free,) behaved very shabbily. The former weighed anchor, about five hours before us, & the latter having started, again anchored lower down in the harbour, for the purpose, as was said of procuring wood; she consequently did not again weigh until late in the evening.

Notwithstanding such advantages in starting, we gained so much on our jealous antagonist the *Cambridge*, that on the succeeding evening, we actually caught her up, & exultingly passing, anchored first in the harbour of Valparaiso. We were surprised to find the whole place in agitation: great political movements had been going on since our absence. The Director, General Freire, had arbitrarily dissolved the Congress; they in return endeavoured to exclude him from the Directorship.

The General was obliged for a short time to evacuate the city; soon after however, the troops, having all declared on his side, he returned, & being thus backed, was enabled to execute summary punishment on his opponents.

No less than eleven or twelve of the principal inhabitants of SantIago, were sentenced to immediate banishment.

Among the rest, the Governor of Valparaiso, being likewise implicated, shared the common fate.

The knowing ones looked on, shook their heads, & pronounc'd "There's something rotten in the State of Denmark."

Having some time before me, I determined once more to visit SantIago: previous however, to my setting off, another play was once more set agoing, amongst the amateurs, & the performance of "The Castle Spectre" produced abundance of applause & commendation from a full & well attended house.

A day or two after, having enlisted two of our Officers, as *Compagnons de voyage*, I made my preparations for setting off to the city, & being in the first place determined to take it leisurely, I bought a horse, conceiving it by far pleasanter, to perform the journey mounted on your own beast, rather than go upon hacks at our former helter skelter pace. My companions followed my example. Accoutered therefore in Ponchas, & *Guasso* [rustic] boots, the travelling dress of the country, behold us all preparing to set off. We wished to sleep at Casa Blanca, & therefore did not start until the afternoon.

As we mounted the hills surrounding Valparaiso, lowering clouds, & a drizzling rain, proclaimed the approach of a wet evening. Shortly after, the rain descended in torrents, & by the time we reached Casa Blanca, we were all drenched to the skin. We had a most miserable moist night in anticipation.

We had hired, & sent on a muleteer, with our trunk; he unfortunately had not yet made his appearance: our only remedy, was partially to strip ourselves, & endeavour to dry, or rather roast & stew our saturated clothes, upon pans filled with charcoal.

Our wretched inn could not boast of possessing a fire-place. We all hied uncomfortable to bed, not much admiring this ominous commencement of our intended trip of pleasure.

Early the next morning we arose, & with long faces, & sluggish hands, arrayed ourselves in garments, still reeking with the last evening's moisture.

Many an imprecation was muttered over obstinate relentless boots, which, shrunk & still well soaked, for some time baffled all exertions to accommodate them to our feet.

These difficulties being at length surmounted we proceeded to horse. The morning had rather an uncomfortable appearance, dark murky clouds, still lowering on the neighbouring hills, menaced us with a repetition of the preceding evening's aqueous disasters, added to which, the rain had freshened & cooled the air so considerably that our clothes, yet damp & uncomfortable, afforded little protection from the sharpened morning breezes.

As the day advanced however, the Sun, after much struggling, succeeded in putting to flight these dense vapours, & the landscape now refresh'd with so much rain, & enjoying the influence of his genial returning presence, exhibited to the eye a more cheerful prospect, & we began to find our ride remarkably pleasant.

At the foot of the Questa de Zapata, we met two or three carriages, conveying to the port, several unfortunate persons, who, having been concerned in the late revolutions, were doomed to be expatriated by Freire, & were now proceeding to embark at Valparaiso. I must own, I could not look upon these unfortunate beings thus about to be torn from their home, friends, & native land, without feelings of deep commiseration for their peculiar hard fate, their greatest crime for the most part, being a diversity of sentiment in political opinion.

At the next posthouse, which was about half way to the city, we refreshed ourselves & baited our horses, & after about an hours rest, we again continued our journey. We were pleased to find that our Nags appeared to feel as fresh as ourselves, for performing the remainder of the jaunt, & I would counsel any person who wishes to ride to the city as a pleasurable excursion, to purchase a horse, upon which he can with great ease & comfort to himself perform the journey in a day & a half; he will also be enabled to see the country round SantIago without incurring further expense for extra horse hire. Our horses, which we found remarkably good, cost us only from 25 to 30 Dollars each. On a former occasion, travelling post, I expended 34 Dollars for the pleasure of going over the ground with greater dispatch.

As, in a previous part of my journal, I have endeavoured to give my reader a faint sketch of the beauties &c., & what may be seen on the road, I now forbear tiring him with tedious repetitions, but merely remark, that the country, having enjoyed the refreshing influence of the late winter months, appeared very much more beautiful & verdant, than on my preceding trip, which was performed during the hottest season of the year.

About four o'clock in the afternoon, we found ourselves at the last post house, on the other side of the Questa de Prao, within about 20 miles of the city: we here again baited our horses, and again set off, hoping to reach the town before the day closed.

As we were passing along, we witnessed an instance of the rapacity of the birds of prey here: two large hawks had mastered a poor lamb, near the road side, & standing over him were busily employed in pecking at his forehead, where they had already inflicted several severe wounds. Luckily our sudden & opportune appearance, saved the little innocent's life, & having dispersed these bloodthirsty despoilers, we performed the part of the Good Samaritan, bound up the poor animals wounds, and conveyed it to a neighbouring farm house. We arrived at the city about Sunset, & our first care was to see our horses (which were somewhat fatigued, having performed that day a journey of about 64 miles) carefully fed, & properly stalled and cleaned.

Ere we left Valparaiso we had all received an invitation from an English merchant (resident in the city, but who had been on a late trip to the port) to consider his house, upon our visiting SantIago, as our head quarters: we therefore now took our friend at his word. He received us with feelings of the most cordial welcome, & in a very short time we found ourselves all boarded & lodged to our very hearts content.

In my former visit to the Capital, I had seen nothing of Chileno society, & now determined to make up for past neglect: I accordingly had provided myself with several letters of introduction to Chileno families: moreover, when last at Valparaiso some months ago I had become acquainted with the Chilian admiral's wife, a most engaging, agreeable woman, who promised on my return to do every thing in her power to render a trip to the city more pleasant.

This lady was now living in SantIago: the next day we proceeded to pay our Chileno visits & deliver our letters of introduction.

We first went to call upon my fair friend the admiral's wife. She seemed very glad to see me again & received us all with the utmost cordiality and attention.

Both myself & companions were much delighted when she introduced to us her mother and four sisters, one of them also married, & two of the remaining three, remarkably pretty, engaging young creatures. Our fair hostess talked French tolerably well: both my companions were middling proficients in Spanish. Altho' not conversant in this language, still I of course understood Portuguese tolerably well, & with this knowledge, I could make myself pretty well understood: moreover here indeed were objects sufficiently attractive to provoke one of most Boeotian capacity to exert his conversational faculties, & I am happy to add, that I very soon, by constant practice, converted my Portuguese acquirement into sufficiently intelligible Spanish, to be enabled to express myself unhesitatingly at least upon most subjects.

But I hasten to take my leave of our new friends, fearing perhaps I may never get thro' the round of visits we had still in contemplation.

We went next to see another family, celebrated in Mrs. Graham's history of Chili: here also were several young ladies, tho' none of them possessing *L'air distingu*[*é*] of our former friends.

The master of the house, upon expressing to him our intention of visiting the Lake of Aculeo, kindly offered us letters of introduction to some part of his family, who resided upon a large estate within a few miles of this beautiful spot: we accordingly determined to be very attentive in our devoirs at the old gentleman's house.

At the next place we visited, a little old gentleman suddenly popt into the room, whose singular appearance and deportment excited our particular attention. He was a little old fashioned looking personage, possessing the most ridiculous countenance imaginable, which was further improved by a curious priggish little wig, having a tortured solitary curl, standing upright immediately from his forehead. His nose and chin, had gradually acquired habits of the strictest intimacy (they very nearly touched each other,) & a brace of twinkling grey eyes peered from beneath a shaggy pair of brows, giving his face a most rogueish & singular expression.

He appeared to be a facetious, jocose little fellow, & we learnt upon inquiry that our friend had formerly been a merchant, from that he had changed to a soldier, from a soldier's profession he had become a lawyer, and in his latter years (it is said he is above 75 years of age) he has become a military chaplain. He was well known to every family at SantIago, & a welcome guest to all: he seemed to have an exquisite taste in judging with discerning eye of female beauty, & possessed a Seraglio of favourites. Some of these more highly in his good graces were called his wives, others were named after various Goddesses. Capt. Hall, in his work on South America, has celebrated the vivacity of this little Priest, & notwithstanding his advancing years, the flame of his wit & good humour, seemed to burn as vividly as ever. Finding we were anxious to extend our list of acquaintances, he promised on the next day, to take us round & introduce us to several families.

In the evening, we went with the Merchant with whom we were

staying, to see a Spanish lady, who had been married to a Frenchman: her family had been educated in France. We were agreeably surprised in being entertained with the most delightful music imaginable. The lady's daughter, a pleasant girl of about eighteen possessed an astonishing musical talent: her style of singing was universally allowed to be nearly equal to that of some of the first proficients on the English boards. Thus amused, our evening passed away most delightfully. What a pity we thought it that so enviable a talent should remain obscured in so remote a place as SantIago, where generally speaking, little taste prevails for music.

Indeed the fine arts are yet in their extreme infancy on this side of South America.

The next day, under the auspices of our merry Mercury, the little Bega, we made a regular round of visits, & were everywhere received with the most cordial welcome.

In the afternoon, we rode out with some part of the Admiral's family, & were invited to their house in the evening, which we passed quite *A l'angloise*, tea being handed round, made by one of the young ladies, reminding us much of good old English customs.

We gaily finished the night's amusements in perfecting ourselves in Spanish country dances. Our mornings, we generally devoted to riding, & as the weather became warm, we found the pleasantest plan was that of taking off one's coat, & supplying its place with a Poncha which, made of silk, or white Cotton, becomes an exceedingly cool & convenient equestrian habit.

Having our own horses thus always at hand, we were enabled to explore the neighbouring country. The heat became rather intense about the middle of the day, when we generally returned, & shifting our riding dresses, prepared to renew our visits.

In Chili, it is a custom, after having once become well acquainted with any family, to continue visiting regularly every day: if you allow any time to elapse, without being thus constant in these duties, you very soon become out of favor.

We determined therefore not to be behind hand in our attentions, & I think were extremely prodigal of our company. The grand attraction however was certainly the Admiral's family, where independent of a greater share of beauty, there was more gayity & less formality prevailing.

Two or three evenings after our arrival, one of my companions, who had been here about four years ago, proposed paying a visit to some old friends of his. These were one of the first families of the place, the head of which however, a man universally loved & esteemed was about to suffer from having taken a share in the late political transactions. He had then ten days allowed him for settling his affairs and was about to leave Chili immediately.

Relying upon our friend's former intimacy, we all set off, & having arrived at the house, were ushered into a splendid drawing room, fitted up in the french & English fashions: this room had a great air of comfort & elegance, was well carpetted, had curtains & Pier Glasses; above all a handsome English mantle piece, & fire place, completely stamped the room with a European air.

Its inmates also reminded us of our own country; they were three young ladies & their mother, rather elegantly dressed, in the English fashion, sitting round a table before the fire (the evenings were still very chilly,) either working, or reading.

On the table were books, work boxes & other housewife articles appertaining to the fair milliners, all which immediately recalled our own fire sides to our recollections.

Here again *l'air distingué* certainly prevailed: indeed the eldest daughter had been the reigning belle of SantIago for the last four years, so long a spell, that I am sure she had now every reason to renounce that distinction which without being partial, I think was latterly usurped by one of the fair ladies amongst our earlier acquaintances in the city. We were received very graciously, & our friend was warmly recognized, but begging his pardon, I think more owing to the rubicund colour of his head, than from any soft impression he might formerly have made on the hearts of our young friends.

As music & dancing were here forbidden owing to the political cloud, which at this time hung over the family, we passed the evening in conversation. The Chileno ladies are the most agreeable creatures possible for young beginners to converse with in a language entirely new to them. They never laugh at you, but with the most patient good humour, listen to, & endeavour to assist you by kindly hoping to divine your thickly enveloped meaning. We certainly murdered the Kings Castilian at a most furious rate, our listeners however tolerated it all with the greatest good humour.

On the 28th news arrived from the port, that the *Maria Isabelle*, bearing the flag of Admiral Blanco, had arrived there. We also learnt that the *Briton* had sailed for Chorillos, a day or two before, & likewise that the *Blossom* had also put into Valparaiso, on her way to Pitcairn's Island. The *Maria Isabelle*, had been the commanding ship of the Chilian blockading squadron off Callao, in which service, she had been employed for the last twelve or fourteen months: her arrival was therefore an event of great importance & felicity to some of our fair friends.

A day or two after, Admiral Blanco appeared in the city, & we, as particular friends of his family were quickly introduced to him. In consequence of his arrival, the Admirals uncle the Marquis of Encallada [Encalada], one of the richest residents in the city, kept open house for several evenings.

Here we were sure of meeting with a most cordial welcome, & almost every evening was spent at the old Gentleman's house, where we generally met with a large party of ladies, Mad. Blanco, and her aimiable sisters generally forming the principal attraction.

The old Marquis possessed one of the most beautiful houses in the city: it was well & elegantly furnished. The master had a great taste for pictures, & his drawing room was hung round with many choice & valuable prints.

Having understood that I amused myself with painting, he took me through a long suite of rooms, entirely hung round with old Pictures: the greater part was certainly a collection of antiquated church rubbish; three or four of them however, originals by Murillo & Vandyck, were unquestionably excellent, & the old gentleman was delighted to find that they attracted so much of my attention.

This is the only person I met with in Chili possessing in any degree, a taste or desire for pictures. As the whole of his collection were very dingy, I promised to send him some Varnish from the port, as also a few prints. I therefore became a great favourite with this venerable amateur.

We spent delightful evenings at his house: a band of music, belonging to one of the regiments, attended constantly, & we gaily pass'd our time in dancing Quadrilles, & Spanish country dances until a late hour.

We now determined to pay a visit to the Lake of Aculeo, & accordingly applied for our promised letters of introduction. One of my companions had also procured a letter from a merchant in the port, to the Marquis of Lareinè [Larrain?], a nobleman possessing the most extensive landed property in Chili. His country house & grounds, being in the direction to the Lake, we were invited by the owner to call upon him there, where he promised to shew us his house & pleasure grounds, which are considered by far the most splendid thing of the kind in Chili.

Early therefore one fine morning, we set off upon this jaunt. We traversed a vast plain surrounding the city: this forms a gentle ascent; it is however so gradual, that you are only reminded of its existence by the bubbling of the different streams of water produced from the melting snows, and which were now proceeding to perform their annual office of irrigating the low grounds about the city. Having pursued our ride for about 12 miles, the monotonous plain, covered with low bushes, loose stones, and here & there patches of short grass, still our only prospect, upon looking back, we found we had imperceptibly made a considerable ascent, & the city, with its churches & convents, now appeared several hundred feet below us.

After about two hours ride, leaving this dreary plain, the country began to assume a livelier character, being now parcelled out and cultivated. Bordering on the road side, we perceived a large farm yard, which we entered in order to beg for a glass of water. Here a grand sheep-shearing was taking place; the women performed the office of disencumbering the animals of their shaggy coats.

We were amused by the dexterity with which several boys assisted; having *Lazo*'s, which are certainly of more utility than our shepherd's crooks they seldom failed in throwing the noose over any particular animal they wished to capture in the flock. Indeed it is not surprizing that they are thus dexterous; the use of the *Lazo*, is a part of the Chilian *Guasso*'s earliest education.

In the streets of Valparaiso, you constantly see little urchins armed with these annoying nooses, greatly to the terror of all quadrupeds, particularly dogs, which, at the whirling of the *Lazo* about the head, instinctively endeavour to make their escape, but seldom with effect, the unerring noose generally embracing some part of their luckless carcase. Another hour's ride, took us to the pass of the river Maypu. This is effected by means of a suspended bridge of hide ropes. The pathway hangs by a vast number of small vertical cords, attach'd (on either bank) to six or eight strongly twisted hide ropes, fastened to large posts on each side of the river, which at this place is about sixty yards across.

The bridge is covered with small sticks, which, in many places, are badly fixed together, & thus rendering the passage hazardous & insecure. The elevation from the river, which runs in a rapid, muddy turbid stream, is about thirty or forty feet; as you proceed across, the elasticity of the materials composing the bridge, cause it to wave up & down, & vibrate in a most unpleasant manner. A day after we passed, a poor horse fell over, & was drowned, owing to the great rapidity of the stream, which at this time was extremely swoln, from the melting of the snows upon the neighbouring Cordillera.

The bed of the river is about half a quarter of a mile wide; there are several petty streams, after you have crossed the bridge, which you are obliged to wade through, up to your horses belly in water.

As you arrive on the other side, & wind round the lowest ridge of the Cordillera, the country begins to wear a most lively & beautiful aspect.

The road still continued very good, but, as the Sun was becoming powerful, & we were becoming hungry, we made up our minds to take refuge in the first decent looking hacienda on the road side, which might present itself to us. We soon perceived a very respectable looking farm house, into the yard of which, we all hied, without the slightest ceremony.

The master of the house who was a captain of militia, & having visited the town that morning, was still arrayed in his military apparel, received us very good-naturedly, & upon being made acquainted with the empty state of our insides, soon set before us a rural repast of bread & excellent fresh butter, hot milk & cheese, all the produce of his own farm, which appeared large & well taken care of.

This modern Cincinnatus was very inquisitive respecting the political state of our country, & the Catholic question: he seemed shrewd & well informed, & shewed us several books on husbandry, translated from English authors into Spanish: these he had lately received from England.

Nature being satiated with a sufficienty of rest & food, we bad[e] adieu to this kind old Patriarch, & proceeded to the hacienda, to which were directed, our letters of introduction. We arrived here about one o'clock, having been much gratified with our ride, which had brought us thro' a country apparently very rich & fruitful, & abounding in fine woody scenery.

We were welcomed to Salinas, (such was the title of the estate,) with much frankness and civility. The family consisted of a Gentleman, his wife, & two male relations. Feeling somewhat fatigued, more owing to the heat of the Sun, than the length of our ride, until dinner time we all enjoyed a refreshing Siesta. This important hour having arrived we sat down to a good plain meal, the heartiness of our reception amply compensating for the absence of delicacies on the table before us.

After dinner, whilst our friends were in their turn enjoying their accustomed Siesta, we prepared ourselves and horses for proceeding to the Lake, which was about fifteen miles from this place.

One of our new friends offered to be our conductor. Our road winded amongst hills, forming a part of the lower ridge of the Cordillera, on either side very thickly wooded & presenting at each moment great diversity of scenery. Our track for some few miles lay thro a thick umbrageous forest: here were large herds of horses quietly grazing; it is a custom in Chili thus to send these animals into the interior, when they become at all jaded or in the slightest degree useless. Here they remain grazing at a very slight expense, until again called into active service.

We arrived at this most delightfully retired Lake just before Sunset; the calm scene before us was inexpressibly beautiful. The Lake, which was a large expanse of pure water, about eight or nine miles in circumference, lay, encircled by the lofty Cordillera, in silvery placidity before us: the beauteous mountain scenery around was reflected on its calm unruffled bosom.

A dreary solitude however seemed to reign around, except when the eye rested upon a few straggling fishermen's cottages, gracing the romantically situated banks.

Wild fowl of every species seemed to revel here in the full enjoyment of uninterrupted peacefulness.

Flocks of Swans, & ducks with varied plumage, glided about in every direction, whilst immense companies of Flamingos with their singular rosy colored feathers, at once stamped the scene with a highly novel & foreign character. After contemplating this enchanting prospect until twilight was approaching, we turned our horses heads homewards, & as we rode along I remarked that the wild flowers & creepers, with which the hedges were thickly mantled, exhaled, as the evening dews heavily descended, the most ineffable sweetness.

As we again approached the house, a burst of voices broke in upon the silence of the evening, & upon entering we perceived that the whole family were occupied at their evenings devotions, in a small chapel adjoining. The master of the house officiated as Priest, & the congregation consisted of his own family, servants & labourers. The service lasted about half an hour, after which we partook of tea & then, discountenancing supper, a most important meal in a Chilian family, we all retired to beds which had been arranged very comfortably for us.

Early on the ensuing morning, we arose, preparing to return to the city: we had previously however arranged with the brother of our host, to conduct us to the seat of the Marquis LaReynes, [Lareine, Larrain?] which was at a short distance from Salinas, & in our way to the city. The morning was beautiful: following our guide, we left the high road, & a short cut thro verdant pasture land well watered, & where innumerable herds of fine cattle were quietly grazing, soon introduced us to the domains of the wealthy Marquis. We soon after came in sight of the house, which had certainly a most imposing air, & from the lofty trees & enclosures around it, appeared more like an English country residence than any thing we had yet seen.

It was Sunday morning & in consequence, a vast number of the neighbouring Peasantry had assembled, & were lounging about on horseback, on the space before the house, awaiting the tolling of the bell to invite them to their morning's devotions. On one side of the house stood a very neat chapel, the interior of which was appropriately fitted up. The Marquis had arrived the preceding evening: upon recognizing his Visiters which cost him some trouble owing to our having adopted the Chilian *Guasso* dress, he begged us to excuse his attendance, until the hour of prayer was over, & in the mean time a servant was ordered to shew us the house, & adjacent grounds, which sufficiently proclaimed the taste & importance of the wealthy proprietor.

The Garden however, which appears to be the pride of the possessor, & envy of the people of the city, did not exactly suit our taste, being laid out in a priggish, formal fashion, with different trees, neatly & carefully cut into various unnatural forms. The Marquis filled up the measure of his attentions by giving us a good breakfast, after which, our curiosity, as well as appetites being satiated we left his house about 12 o'clock, prudently resolving to be if possible in the city by three, the accustomed dinner hour of our kind host, the merchant. Instinctively, about this time, we found ourselves at our old quarters, & in the afternoon were enabled to be present at the Tacamar. Here as I have said before, the whole of the "beau monde" of SantIago resorted of an afternoon, particularly on Sundays & fête days, when all the beauty & fashion of the city influenced by the charms of pedestrian recreation, appeared to frequent these favored walks. The ladies were invariably seen, gaily, & tastefully dressed; I cannot forbear adding that in decorative accomplishments, they far surpass the men of this country, nor do these latter, in any degree partake of the graceful & agreeable manners, of the fairer part of the Chileno creation.

I must not forget remarking a still more fascinating prospect which was here exhibited. The neighbouring Cordillera, thickly mantled in a garb of snow, present at all times to a strangers notice, an effect inexpressibly grand & attractive. From these gay walks however, at the calm hour of sunset, this lovely scene is considerably improved.

At this time of the year, the Sun generally retires to rest, surrounded by a blaze of blushing glory, from which the adjacent Andes acquire a roseate hue, impossible to be imagined or described, but which a stranger is never fatigued in gazing upon, & it is delightful to observe, as the bright orb of day, thus gloriously deserts the horizon, the various cold grey tints, which gradually spread over the face of the landscape and ultimately dispossess the mountains of their beauteous borrowed blushes. So I have seen the hectic blush transiently mantling the cheek of a consumptive beauty, for a few moments lighting up the countenances with a clear roseate colour, & then again leaving it pale, wan, & statue like, as before.

About this tranquil time also, the vesper bells of the neighbouring convents toll forth the evening hour of prayer, & upon looking about, you perceive an instantaneous adorative movement among the gay surrounding circle: the hum of conversation ceases for a few moments; all cross themselves, & with heads uncovered, address their evening thanksgivings to the blessed Mary.

> "Ave Maria! blessed be the hour!
> The time, the clime, the spot, where I so oft
> Have felt that moment in its fullest power
> Sink o'er the earth so beautiful and soft,
> While swung the deep bell in the distant tower
> Or the faint dying day-hymn, stole aloft,
> And not a breath crept thro' the rosy air,
> And yet the forest leaves seem'd stirr'd with prayer."

These feelings in unison with the heavenly prospect gradually fading from your sight, were sufficient I think to provoke the most thoughtless to a few minutes meditation.

The Government of Chili had long been preparing an armament to send against the isle of Chiloe. This was now almost ready, & it was decided that the whole Chilian naval force, should in a few days leave Valparaiso for this island: 2,400 Soldiers destined for the expedition were to be headed by the Director in person.

Admiral Blanco had the command of the naval force, & in consequence decided upon leaving SantIago very soon, in order to expedite the equipments at the port. Madame Blanco, & her two sisters (luckily the two prettiest) were to accompany him.

About this time we also discovered that we had seen sufficient of the city, & began therefore to make similar arrangements for a retrograde movement. The Admiral and his family left the city on the 21st & on the following day myself & one other of my companions fixed upon returning also; our remaining friend was bent upon an excursion to the snowy peaks of the Andes, a region by far too cold & chilly for the rest of the party's inclinations.

Being determined to see our friends safe out of the town, we accompanied them on horseback, for the first four miles. Their carriage was one of the country, badly constructed, & in which the sitters seemed to ride most uncomfortably. Fate taking pity on their persons, soon caused a mighty revolution, for in passing a rough, stony part of the road (o! blessed blacksmith) the iron work sustaining the springs, suddenly gave way, & we had the supreme felicity of handing out unhurt the precious part of the clumsy vehicles burden, & which was now rendered unfit to pursue the journey; luckily, it was yet sufficiently strong to afford a conveyance back to the town for the disconsolate travellers.

This ominous commencement afforded the greatest mirth to the whole party, which on our side was converted into a very agreeable feeling of pleasure when Mad. Blanco, hearing that we had intended starting on the following morning, proposed that we should accompany her family to the port.

We, as may be imagined, readily assented to this new arrangement, & it was then determined that on the ensuing morning, we should all start about eight o'clock. We spent the remaining evening in paying farewell visits. The family, to whom our rubicund headed friend had introduced us also intended in a few days to leave SantIago for the port. Early on the succeeding morning we prepared for our return jaunt. The state of the weather, which had been warm & sultry, again threatened us with a renewal of our former pluvious disasters, continued rain having poured down during the whole preceding night. The morning however turned out mild & agreeable, & the past moisture had delightfully watered the previous dusty roads, "and nature smil'd revived".

Our place of rendezvous was the Marquis of Encallada's house, where we found our friends busily preparing for their journey.

A convenient English barouche, sufficiently large to accommodate the whole party was now substituted for the wretched vehicle of the preceding day. What would Captain Hall say now could he behold such a carriage drawn by four horses, posting it down to Valparaiso: at the uncivilized period of the writing of his book, the reader learns that vehicles of no description except Carritas drawn by oxen, travelled from the city to the port.

The carriage being light, & the roads good we were enabled to proceed at a hand canter until we arrived at the first posthouse, where our company alighted in order to procure fresh horses. The manner of furnishing Post horses in Chili is very different to our customs.

The horses are all hired at the place you first start from (our friends had three relays, or twelve animals) & those not employed, are led in droves by a Peon, at some distance before you; in this way however, it is impossible to have your horses very fresh after the first stage: moreover those taken from the Carriage are obliged to wave the necessity & comfort of rest, & are trotted along, in order to take their share of the draught as it next revolves to them. Having passed about half an hour at the post house, which consists of only a few huts, possessing no accommodation for travellers, we again resumed our journey. The Questa de Prao was before us: One of the ladies now mounted on horseback, her own beast, having accompanied us, already saddled for the occasion. The road over this hill, which is about 2000 feet in height is broad & well formed, & cut into several zigzags to facilitate its ascent, which in some parts is very steep: the carriage therefore proceeded at a very slow rate, & above two hours elapsed, ere we arrived at the base of the mountain on the other side. The enjoyment however of contemplating the beautiful prospect encompassing us, insensibly curtailed its length, & I was pleased to observe that our fair equestrian companion was fully alive to the attractive natural beauties thus surrounding her.

The Chilian ladies have a great passion for flowers, & in their woods & mountains, these sweet children of Flora, abound in the greatest luxuriance & variety; it became therefore our duty to supply our fair friends with numberless wild bouquets, culled from the adjacent fields, & sides of the road as we passed gaily along.

While on the subject of flowers, I cannot forbear remarking a custom which seems universally prevalent in Chili.

Upon paying a visit, you are scarcely seated, ere one of the ladies of the house retires from the apartment, & having entered the inner quadra (in SantIago, there is to each house a quadra or square which, laid out with various plants is solely devoted to horticulture) presently returns laden with the choicest flowers: these she carefully prepares by removing the thorns or superabundance of leaves, & then distributes them in the most graceful manner to her visiters.

It is also expected that the Gentlemen should frequently decorate their buttonholes with bouquets to be enabled in their turn to distribute such innocent & sensible proofs of amity & regard.

Another change of horses having taken place, we continued our route; it had been previously determined that we should dine and sleep at Bustamente, the second post house, about half way to the port, & in furtherance of this plan, the Admirals aid-de-camp, had been dispatched on the previous day, to bespeak beds, & prepare the post house for so many illustrious guests.

Our road still continued uncommonly good, & we advanced at a rapid pace. By the way of variety Admiral Blanco (who by the bye, is one of the most agreeable & polite men I have seen in Chili) proposed mounting my horse, & resigning to me his seat in the carriage. This change was of course assented to without the slightest objection on my part; indeed I found my destiny greatly improved, & seated by the side of a delightful girl, methought all nature & the landscape around appeared more lovely, & had the Admiral taken possession of my horse for the remainder of the journey, not one repining murmur should have escaped my lips.

Just as twilight was commencing we reach'd our destined auberge, & until dinner, or rather supper time arrived, my companion & myself endeavoured to make ourselves useful by superintending the luggage from the carriage and unpacking the band boxes, whilst two of the ladies undertook the arrangement of the sleeping chambers (which were rustic enough in their way) & actually had sufficient complaisance to prepare our beds with their own delicate hands.

A hot substantial supper soon smok'd on the genial board, & our naval friend & entertainer having had sufficient foresight & proper feeling to introduce into the recesses of the carriage amongst the band boxes, a small case of excellent claret, we continued to make a tolerable meal.

Shortly after we all separated to enjoy the balmy influence of a good nights rest, so necessary to the ladies at least after their day's fatigue.

We were all to start at Sunrise on the following morning, at which time we arose, & found the ladies habited & already preparing their luggage for the carriage. We determined to breakfast about 15 miles from the present stage.

Our horses appeared fresh, & the whole party animated by the beauty of a lovely morning.

By the time all was ready, the bright messenger of day had gradually advanced somewhat on his journey, but as yet, had only partially dispersed the morning mists, which still hung curtained upon the lofty peaks of the surrounding Cordillera, seeming like barriers to separate them from the gay sunny world below.

About ten o'clock we again halted to breakfast, which we partook of in the most rural manner possible. Our eatables were taken to a neighbouring enclosure, upon the verge of a hill, skirted by a fine wood. Our carpet was velvetty turf, whilst the branches of the surrounding trees festooned with air plants & sweet smelling creepers formed a delightful protecting canopy from the rays of the Sun.

We now recommenced our journey & soon after arrived at the foot of the Questa de Zapata; here one of the ladies again mounted the side-saddled horse finding this by far the most pleasant manner of passing over these precipitate mountains.

They have in Chili a curious manner for preventing the carriages from descending the hills too rapidly.

One of the Peons takes his horse from the traces and attaching his Lazo (a Chilian Guasso never travels without this necessary piece of furniture affixed to his racou or Guasso saddle,) to the hind part of the carriage, his horse, which is well practised in the duty, backs all the way down & completely performs the service of a drag-wheel. The Lazos are made of green hide, very strong, & fully capable of bearing this strain, without danger of giving way.

At the Valparaiso side of the questa, the lady again dismounted from her horse, & we now proceeded until within about twenty miles of the port. At this last place, we remained only sufficient time to procure another relay of horses, & our active & useful aid-de-camp, being again dispatched to prepare a dinner at the Admiral's house, we jogged on, & just before Sunset, the bay of Valparaiso & the shipping suddenly appeared to our view from the lofty hills over-hanging them, & down which the road descends in a zigzag direction.

A traveller is generally well pleased, as the sight of his native home, town, or even ship, proclaims the completion of his journey: with myself & companion it proved somewhat different, & an unaccount-able feeling assured us that we could have prolonged the journey with pleasure for several leagues more, particularly if the Admiral would have been complaisant enough to have again taken to equestrian exercise.

Our carriage drew up at a large house in the Almendral, the building of which had been very recently finished; indeed the rooms, which were large & airy, were still in a most pristine state; here however, notwithstanding the lack of furniture, & appropriate decoration, we managed a successful attack upon a most excellent dinner, & soon after, having thus safely housed our agreeable friends, we bad[e] them adieu, & returned on board much pleased with our late trip & visit to the city.

10
Farewell to Valparaíso

We found all our messmates quite well, & some of them not a little pleased with our promise of introducing them to a pleasant Chileno family, there being, as I have said before, very little society of the kind at the port. During the remaining time we stayed here, we found notwithstanding we possessed some very pleasant English society that our Santiago friends, proved a delightful acquisition to us: really, some of our officers, who had seldom quitted the ship during our absence, were now very constant in their visits to the shore.

There were a troop of horses kept in the livery stables at the port, any of which, upon his masters mounting him, proceeded with an instinctive expeditious movement towards the Almendral. I cannot divine the attraction: perhaps the scent of the balmy country air coming from that direction, was their sole enticement. With such pleasant objects to commune with, we of course made great progress in Spanish: our friends were passing kind in assisting us in our infantine linguistical endeavours, & how true these lines of [the poet] Lord Byron's are many of the *Blonde*'s officers can testify.

> "'Tis pleasing to be school'd in a strange tongue
> By female lips and eyes—that is, I mean,
> When both the teacher and the taught are young,
> As was the case at least where I have been;
> They smile so when one's right, and when one's wrong
> They smile still more."

It will not be apropos perhaps to pursue the quotation any further, truth however may still cling to his Lordship's succeeding poetical conceptions.

We now began to think seriously of taking leave, & in eight or ten days the *Blonde* was destined to pursue her voyage to England.

In the meantime I had a most arduous undertaking to commence: having unwarily promised to paint a lady's picture, when at the city, I was now called upon to fulfil this fascinating but dangerous engagement.

I was thus occupied for several days & became enabled from my constant attendance, to form a more accurate judgment respecting the manners of living adopted by Chilian families, which is beginning amongst the first societies, to assume very much the English customs.

Since our last visit, a large French force had arrived at Valparaiso, no less than six or eight men of war were riding at anchor here. They consisted of the *Maria Therese*, sixty gun Frigate commanded by Admiral Rosamel, the *Thetis* Frigate & *L'Esperance* corvette (which two latter vessels, were about making the tour of the world) with several smaller vessels & shore ships, which in their service are fitted up as men of war. These vessels composed a formidable armament, & so many French flags thus flying in the port, at the same time, were regarded by the Chilians with somewhat a jealous eye: the French are by no means popular on this side [of] Cape Horn.

The preparations against Chiloe, being now finally completed, the expedition set sail from Valparaiso on the 1st Dec.: their squadron consisted of the Frigate *Maria Isabelle*, several sloops, & brigs of war, together with Transports for the convenience of the troops.

It is to be hoped that the present armament will now be more fortunate: their last attack upon the island was attended by a severe repulse, & I think considering the disaffection reigning throughout the present equipment (owing to the arrears of both soldiers & sailors, not having been made good to them, for many, many months) its success is certainly very dubious.

Previous to our departure, & in order to throw an eclat on our final adieus, we proposed giving a ball on board. Under the direction of our Officers, the entertainment was managed, with that taste & good arrangement, peculiar to so gallant a ship. All the principal families, Chileno, as well as English, attended on the occasion, together with the officers of the different French men of war. I am sure I may be allowed to affirm, notwithstanding my being a party concerned, that no gayety of the kind has afforded to the fair residents of Valparaiso an evening of greater gratification & enjoyment.

Of course the Admiral's family made a conspicuous figure: one of the young ladies having a pretty taste for music, had presented me with several waltzes, the production of her composing fancy. These had been practised by our band, and were now played greatly to the satisfaction & honour of the fair musician.

I cannot forbear relating an unhappy event which took place on this festive night. Amongst our guests, were a large party of young ladies, called Carrera, a title ranked amongst the first in Chili, & a name & family famous in the late revolutions. Many of its members had fallen victims to the passed disorderly state of the times.

The only surviving brother of these ladies, resided with his father upon the family estate a few miles distant from Valparaiso. He was known to be a young man of a dark & desperate character, insomuch, that the hapless father would painfully be obliged to caution the stranger, who had just perhaps partaken of the hospitality his house afforded to put himself upon his guard against the lawless attempts of his own son, who was frequently known to infest the roads at the head of a formidable banditti.

The night previous to our ball, this desperate youth had been engaged in some plundering excursion; the party assaulted concerted a speedy & fatal planned scheme of revenge, & on the following night during our festivities, the surgeon was called out to attend upon young Carrera who had been attacked whilst sleeping under a tree, with a servant beside him: the latter was immediately dispatched. His master however, having received seven desperate wounds, & left for dead, upon returning animation, had strength sufficient to crawl to his father's house, whither the Surgeon now immediately proceeded.

This was a sad tale for the poor sisters upon their return from their evenings diversions. On the succeeding day I again saw the Surgeon: the unhappy Carrera expired that evening from his wounds, the least of which the Surgeon considered mortal.

It is astonishing to think how fatally certain & dexterous these people are in the use of a Knife, which is resorted to upon the slightest provocation: the wound is generally inflicted with deadly precision upon some vital part. Two of our sailors, & also several belonging to the other men of war on the station, have, during our short stay here, fallen victims to the hasty vindictive passions of these people.

The Surgeon attended the death bed of this Carrera, & gave me a curious account of the superstitious, bigoted conduct of the monks; ministering during the last moments of the expiring man.

Notwithstanding he was speechless, & insensible, the blind senseless fathers at his bed side were assiduously requiring, in the words addressed to the guilty Beaufort,

"Hold up thy hand, make signal of thy hope",

in order that they might administer absolution and the extreme unction.

In vain they sollicited, & were already exclaiming "He dies, and makes no sign", when a sudden paroxysm, agitating the almost lifeless person of the unhappy sufferer, caused the hand which was locked in that of one of the Priests, to impart a convulsive pressure: this was joyfully hailed as the dying Penitential signal, & the last rites of the Roman Catholic religion were accordingly duly administered.

On the 3d Dec the trying & affecting moment of separation with our fair Valparaiso friends arrived, & early the next morning we weighed anchor.

As our noble Frigate gradually expanded her bellying canvass to the morning breezes, many a fluttering signal of responsive kerchief from the balconies of our Almendral friends, proclaimed the sad & heart rending interest excited by our departure.

I cannot forbear remarking the touching conduct of one of my messmates; standing upon the taffarel [tafferel], & partially occupied in setting sail, he would at one time lustily sing out "Mizen top there; Light up your topsail clue lines", or some other necessary order, & would then ever and anon direct his restless & softened gaze once more towards the aforesaid balcony,

> "as he hearty wav'd
> His last adieu, & loosening every sheet,
> Resign'd the spreading vessel to the wind."

But I must hurry over this affecting scene before it becomes too touching, & proceed to relate how a prosperous breeze soon carried us to Coquimbo, which little digression from our course the Captain was tempted to make, in order to afford to the Director of the Anglo Chilian mining association of Coquimbo an opportunity of returning thither.

11
Coquimbo and the Anglo-Chilean Mines

This place is about 65 leagues to the northward of Valparaiso. It is a general remark that the farther you proceed to the northward on the Chilian & Peruvian coasts, the more sterile & unproductive is the face of the country.

The neighbourhood of Coquimbo looks dreary & desolate, even after the barren looking country about Valparaiso.

The ship came to an anchor towards the southern part of the bay, about half a mile from the shore: the anchorage which is very good, is sheltered from the northerly winds by several small islets. It was determined that we should remain at this place for four or five days only. In the afternoon, I went on shore with several of my mess-mates, purposing to visit Serena, the capital of this district, & where resided our mining friend, who gave us all a carte blanche to his house. The port of Coquimbo itself is merely an insignificant village, built near a ledge of rocks, which forms a shelter for the bay, & where ships land their cargoes.

Hearing of the arrival of a Frigate, the neighbouring Guassos flocked down to the beach, with their horses for our use, charging a Dollar for a ride to the town of Serena, which is about nine miles distant from the port.

We were all soon mounted. Our road for several miles lay along the sea beach, the country around presenting a blank space of Sand interspers'd with shrubs.

When within about 2 miles from the town, the scenery becomes more diversified, and as you enter the town itself you cannot fail in being struck with its fresh and pleasant appearance.

It is situated on a gentle acclivity: on one side is a fine sandy bay, on the other, a beautiful & fertile valley, thro' which runs the river of Coquimbo, & empties itself into the sea. The streets as in all Chilian towns are built at right angles, & the lively verdure of the fig trees, palms, orange & olive trees, abundantly flourishing in the vicinity of the town, impart to it a luxuriant & cultivated appearance.

Our mining friend furnished us all to the number of eight or ten persons, with board & lodging, & proposed on the following morning, that we should take a jaunt into the interior of the country, to see his mines which are situated about forty miles from the town, in the vicinity of the lower ridge of the Cordillera. On the ensuing morning therefore, a large party of us prepared for this jaunt: the country people, hearing of our intended trip, offered us, as on the preceding day their horses, for the use of which they demanded 5 Dollars. To a person unaccustomed to so rude a seat, a Guasso saddle forms a poor apology for one of English manufacture.

The load these saddles assure to the poor horse, is quite enormous. Having first placed on the animals back, a wooden pack-saddle, about eight different cloths, each having an appropriate appellation, are put on: then comes as the last covering, a sheepskin, dyed in general a dark blue. This apparatus is called a *racou*, & until accustomed to it, proves a warm & uncomfortable seat, & not at all calculated to administer to the ease of a forty miles ride. It however possesses one great advantage: so many cloths constitute a good bed at night should the traveller be no better accommodated. Large blocks of wood, hollowed out to receive your toe, serve as stirrups. These accoutrements are expensive. I paid 30 Dollars at Valparaiso, for a complete Guasso equipment of the commonest description. Our mining friend, (a most worthy fellow) undertook to supply the whole party with an ample quantity of Prog [provisions]. As we left the town, we descended into the valley, & were obliged to ford the river Coquimbo, which becoming rapid and swoln, from the continual melting snows, proved rather a hazardous adventure.

In a few days more, the river would be so much more swoln & rapid, as to prevent people from passing for some weeks without imminent danger.

On the opposite side, about five miles from the town, a most beautiful view presented itself to us. Between us & the town we had just left, lay a rich valley, irrigated by the river Coquimbo, whose waters formed a variety of doublings & fanciful windings, sometimes glittering amongst willows which fringed its borders, & again disappearing amidst the bright green foliage which in some places surrounded its banks, or making an azure sweep in full view round a slope of verdant meadow land: a distant ridge of undulating blue mountains, bounded the beauteous landscapes.

Leaving this scene, our road now led us through vast plains, of low brushwood, the ride rendered somewhat unpleasant by attendant clouds of dust, & sharp loose stones scattered over the road: these the horses scrambled over at an amazing pace, notwithstanding none of their hoofs are protected by shoes. The parallel roads mentioned by Capt. Hall, are very visible in the distance, but as you approach, what you at first took for a road, appears nothing but a large space disencumbered of grass & shrubs, & abounding in loose stones of all sizes.

Having left these plains, we now entered amongst the mountains. The scenery here was very monotonous and tiresome, and the foots pace at which we were obliged to creep up a desolate Quebrada or ravine, reaching for about 20 miles, produced in us a longing to come to our journey's end. The last six miles of our ride proved more interesting. Issuing from these disagreeable Quebradas, our road now commanded a grand but wild & gloomy prospect: deep dreary vallies, branched out for many miles in various windings beneath our feet. These were bounded by the gigantic Cordillera rearing their lofty spiral forms in all the savage grandeur of the most profound solitude and gloomy desertion.

About five o'clock we arrived at the mining territories. They presented to our view, a large mountain, over the face of which, were scattered a great number of small huts, the residences of the different mining agents, & near which were excavations & heaps of stones: these impregnated with the silver ore, were beat up in small pieces, in order to undergo the process of amalgamation. The knowledge that these districts contained silver, was accidentally discovered about three years since by several wood cutters, one of whose party casually observing a specimen of silver ore, conveyed it to the city. Immediately after the mining operations commenced with great vigour; the wood cutters had a portion of land awarded to them, which being too poor to work they immediately sold, & the whole population of Serena, since that period, has appeared wholly wrapt up in mining speculation. How very true and appropriate to the general feeling existing in these mining districts are the remarks of Dr. Robertson, in his history of South America. Treating of portions of land allotted to mining adventurers, he says

> Invited by the facility with which such grants are obtained and encouraged by some striking examples of success in this line of

COQUIMBO, CHI

"Horses . . . a Dollar for a rid

R. D. delt. 1826.

adventure, not only the sanguine and bold, but the timid and diffident enter upon it with astonishing ardour.

With vast objects in view, fed continually with hope, and expecting every moment that fortune will unveil her secret stores, and give up the wealth which they contain to their wishes, they deem every other occupation insipid and uninviting.

The charms for this pursuit, like the rage for deep play, are so bewitching, and take such full possession of the mind, as even to give a new bent to the natural temper. Under its influence, the cautious become enterprising, and the covetous profuse!

Again how very justly he remarks,

For it is observed, that if any person once enters this seducing path, it is almost impossible to return; his ideas alter, he seems to be possessed with another spirit; visions of imaginary wealth are continually before his eyes, and he thinks, and speaks, and dreams of nothing else.

Two or three small wretched looking huts on the side of a barren mountain, now proclaim'd our arrival at the Anglo Chilian mining district. A couple of German miners were resident here, & superintended the excavations, having under them six or eight Peons to carry on the more arduous employment of digging out the ore.

Our first care was to disburthen our horses of their pack saddles, & set them free on the thrifty plain, where they were no doubt puzzled to procure their well earned supper, Dame nature I suppose conceiving that the interior richness of the soil, amply compensated for its exterior sterility, & lack of herbage.

Our case was widely different: several well furnished hampers spoke volumes to our famished feelings, & whilst these were unpacking, we explored the riches concealed in the bowels of our mother earth.

Several excavations had been made, into one of which, we descended, reaching about 20 feet below the surface. The vein of silver appeared uncommonly rich & abundant: it ran in breadth & depth about 25 inches & as we had procured a hammer, we soon filled our pockets with specimens.

The duty of filling our stomachs likewise with specimens of a more digestive nature, now occupied the remainder of the evening.

The Group which presented itself inside the hut, would have produced a picture worthy of the incomparable Wilkie. Our hut consisted of a few mats, branches of trees, palm leaves, & straw rudely put together: from the pristine cieling hung a lamp throwing its dim light on several well contented individuals, busily employed in discussing the merits of various pies, & joints of meat, which lay in disorganized confusion upon a table in the centre. These were flank'd by a regiment of bottles, some of whose hollow stomachs, already proclaimed their further inutility. On a bench somewhat removed from this active consuming discussion were seated three Chilian visiters, whom our friend assured us were the greatest villains upon earth: one of these had been the former proprietor of the mine, & it was thought political to be monstrous civil to himself & companions, notwithstanding their aimiable characters. To complete the picture, one of the German miners with guitar in hand, amused us with several comic songs, at the same time accompanying himself upon his instrument with many a grotesque grimace. The background was filled up with the swarthy countenances of the lower miners, who were allowed to enter & enjoy the inexpressible pleasure of seeing us feasting ourselves. As the glassy regiment gradually poured forth their rubicund treasures, many a toast was pledged, by either party.

I cannot forbear remarking an unlucky mistake which occurred during this original entertainment. Desirous of shewing our goodwill to the Director of Chili, & affection for our guests the villains, we propos'd drinking the General's health, & success to the Chilian arms in bumpers of exhilirating Punch.

The toast was given, but alas! we found our nectareous beverage, converted into the sourest vinegar, that liquor having been substituted in mistake by our blundering Ganymede. We soon after got rid of our Chilian guests, & wrapping ourselves in our Ponchos, composed our persons to sleep. The next morning we returned again to Serena, not however feeling our minds very much impressed with the teeming richness of the Anglo Chilian mines, in which I should hesitate very much in purchasing a share. Lord Byron I think received an excellent & appropriate answer from a Cornish miner, respecting the prospect of future remuneration in working these mines. "I liken it" said the miner, "to a man who has been told that a guinea may be found deposited in a neighbouring block of granite; he diligently sets to work, but unfortunately expends five & thirty shillings in extracting the golden treasure from its stony tenement." In compliment to the arrival of the *Blonde*, (a grand occurrence at Coquimbo) our friends the Anglo Chilians gave a ball during the time we were there.

A vast assemblage honoured us with their presence; examples of beauty however were very scarce; many of the ladies seemed like our quondam friends the Sandwich Queens, to revel in a multiplicity of fat: all of them were somewhat below par in good breeding. Perhaps the company of our SantIago friends, & the impression of their aimiability still fresh upon our minds now rendered us somewhat squeamish & particular.

The next day a party of these well fleshed ladies proposed visiting the ship; one of our Lieutenants undertook to be charioteer, & conducted them to the port in safety, in a carriage or light waggon drawn by two horses.

On his return, in passing a huge stone, perhaps the boundary or "terminus" of other days, not having I suppose practised much at the Olympic games

> "Perchance, the reins forsook the drivers hand
> And turn'd too short, he tumbled on the strand"

& dire to relate, the waggon parting from its axle trees, & wheels, overturned, at the same time acting as a covering for its former precious load, as you may perchance have seen a flock of luckless birds entrapped by the sudden fall of a basket, or some other ingenious school-boy expedient. Luckily, the ladies being very fat, & the ground very soft, no injury whatever was sustained. On the 13th Decr. we took our final leave of the shores of South America, merely intending to lay off the isle of Chiloe for a few hours to ascertain if it had surrendered to the Chilian squadron. When in the latitude of this place, a sudden favorable wind sprung up, which the Captain felt very unwilling to part with; we therefore gave up all idea of visiting Chiloe, & proceeded on our passage round the Horn.

12

Around Cape Horn, to St. Helena, and Journey's End

Favorable breezes again accompanied our fortunate vessel, & in the course of ten days we repass'd this boisterous rendezvous of storms: indeed like the ship of the sage Ulysses, all adverse winds seem completely vanished from the latitudes we have hitherto been traversing. I heartily trust their pent up fury will not be vented forth in a violent tempestuous* Euroclydon just as we are about nearing our native shores. Having rounded the Cape, our track lay exactly in the direction of an island discovered by La Rochein [Roché] & called Isle of Grandi [Isla Grande]. This island is minutely described by its discoverer, but no other ship has since been fortunate enough to catch a glimpse of it.

On the 8th January, just after mid-day, the ships reckoning having been brought into the Captain, placed us immediately in the situation when the above said island ought to have been found. The day was uncommonly thick & hazy: it was an extraordinary circumstance. Lord Byron was just affirming that if such a place existed, we ought now to be almost upon it, when we were interrupted by the sudden entrance of the master, who declared that high land was visible very close to us immediately upon our starboard bow. All were in a moment busily engaged in putting the ship about, when upon taking a less hurried view of this sudden formidable coast, the Spectre in the form of high land, proved to our great disappointment an immense iceberg, & very soon afterwards, several smaller ones were seen, also very near us. One of our Officers who by the bye, is extremely short sighted, upon examining the supposed land, before its identity was discovered, clearly laid out to us, the whole line of coast in the intermediate spaces of the icebergs.

Having advanced so far to the Northward, we did not dream of such inhospitable neighbours, & providential was it indeed that the rencontre took place in broad day, as we were steering directly upon this formidable impediment. We now changed our course, & soon lost sight of these chilly looking mountains & on the 23d Jany., after a prosperous voyage of six weeks, we made the island of St. Helena. What must have been Napoleon's feelings on first viewing

* vide note in Mant's bible, Acts, Verse 14, Chapter 27.

THE *BLONDE* IN THE SOUTH ATLANTI[C]
"This . . . formidable coast . . . proved . . . an immense iceberg

from the deck of the *Bellerophon* the dreary outline of his future resting place.

The island from the sea as we coasted along to windward of it appeared one entire mass of gigantic rock piled upon rock, without one single spot of verdure to deck their bleak summits or rugged sides. On some of the highest peaks, perched like eagles nests, were several signal houses & flag staffs.

As we advanced towards the anchorage, we were suddenly & agreeably surprised as the valley of St. James's opened to our view the neat little town of that name. On either side were stupendous barren rocks, their summits crown'd with very strong batteries: from one, to the right of the town, the moment we cast anchor, which was within a quarter of a mile from the shore, a salute of 13 Guns, was promptly fired.

The neat & regular appearance of the town, the Governor's house with beautiful green trees around its precincts, the elegant little church, the neat & white wash'd buildings form a fine contrast with the rude bold rocks frowning abruptly on either side.

The island appears of volcanic origin, & many parts particularly the rocks overhanging the sea, recalled to our minds the dark red vari[e]gated cliffs of the Galapagos & of some parts of the Sandwich Islands. The town is defended in addition to the fortified heights with a row of 32 Pounders, stretching in front, & on a level with it.

Immediately after anchoring I accompanied Lord Byron to the shore. After having resided so long in the slovenly mal-arranged towns of South America, I felt much struck at the neatness, cleanliness & decidedly Eng: air of comfort presiding everywhere here.

The town consists of one wide regular street, which branches off into two others, rather narrower, one towards the East, leading to the country in that direction, & the other to the upper part of the valley. The eye becomes gladdened & revived by the appearance of a beautiful verdure clothing the distant inland hills.

About 11 o'clock, the Governor Genl. Walker, arrived from Plantation House, his seat in the country, & we immediately paid him a visit. We were most graciously received & introduced by him

to his lady, who had also accompanied him to the town. We found him a remarkably pleasant engaging person, & felt still more satisfied with our reception when the General invited us to his house in the country, at the same time begging the Captain to bring with him any of his friends he pleased from the Frigate. Horses were ordered at 5 o'clock to convey us to Plantation house.

Two different roads lead you from the town into the interior of the island, the one on the right or western side, called Ladder Hill, a well cut zigzag carriage road, & a safe and easy ascent, & the other to the left of the valley, called Sidepath, and leading to the eastward of the island. Both these roads are rendered secure by strong walls built on the side nearest the precipice, & are perfectly safe for carriages. The Governor comes to, & returns from town in one drawn by six horses; many of the inhabitants possess likewise vehicles of some description: the passing waggons, carts, & teams of horses, continually remind you of England.

As we mounted Ladder hill, & advanced more into the interior, we were sensibly struck with the sudden magic change on the face of the surrounding prospect. On all sides are neat country houses, their precincts highly cultivated, & encircled with oaks, & plantations of fir trees, which latter flourish very abundantly here. Rich well clothed vallies, & lively green pasture land, form the interior aspect of the island, which looks doubly verdant and beautiful from the contrast afforded by the barren rugged rocks, surrounding the coast.

We soon arrived at the environs of Plantation house, & from a path, winding amongst a grove of trees, we were suddenly conveyed to the habitation itself, which has all the appearance of a beautiful country residence in England.

A large party had been convened to meet us & we sat down to table no less than six & twenty in number. The next morning, I arose early in order to explore the neighbouring estate. To one like myself, who had resided so many years distant from England & all its comforts, this sudden metamorphosis had a sensible effect, & I wandered delighted along beautiful shaded paths & thick umbrageous woods, where European & tropical vegetation vied with each other in

PLANTATION HOUSE, ST. HELENA
"All the appearance of a beautiful country residence in England"

leafy luxuriance, listening with all the charm of novelty to the note of the blackbird or distant echoing call of the pheasant & black-cock, (these birds have been sent from England & thrive very well here) & almost fancying myself once more transported to my native country.

The well regulated house, respectful servants, adjoining delightful grounds, together with the agreeable owners of the place all tend to favour & strengthen this pleasing delusion.

I occupied myself a short time in taking a sketch of the house & its environs, & then proceeded to the stables & coach-houses: the former were occupied by about 26 horses all kept for the accommodation of the General & his guests at the India company's expense, who certainly are extremely liberal in their way of doing things. In the latter were three carriages. General Walker, is I believe allowed about £1800 per annum: the whole of his expenses attending the establishment of Plantation house, which (considering how very dear everything is in the island) must be enormous, are defrayed by the East India company.

Nothing can exceed the beneficence, hospitality, & kindness of the old General & his lady: they are uncommonly popular & well liked here.

We were all treated with particular attention, & repeated invitations were sent to all the officers & midshipmen on board: It may therefore be imagined that Plantation house, became the headquarters to very many of the *Blonde*'s. I remained there from the day I landed until our departure.

Below Plantation House, are the places of worship resorted to by the Chinese, of which nation there are a great number in the island.

The roof of their temple was ornamented with wooden images of Dolphins, & other grotesque figures: before its doors were erected several long poles with a few sticks placed crossways on the top. Upon entering, you find yourself opposite a sort of shrine, which reminds you of the altar of a small Roman Catholic chapel.

Instead of waxen candles however, you are here treated with pieces of stick, rolls of paper with Chinese characters upon them, & a great deal more of unintelligible trumpery attendant on either side. In the midst instead of a Virgin Mary, you have the figure of a fat contented jolly old Deity ycleped *Jos* [Joss]; on the left of this god, stands his mistress, supposed by these worshippers to be the mother of mankind. His right hand is occupied by the figure of a most diabolical familiar, whose demoniac grin proclaims him the destroyer, & mortal enemy of our race. Like the direful Parca, in his hands he holds the fatal shears to curtail our human destinies. Before this sainted trio, burns a perpetual fire. Lighted odoriferous incense gratify their immortal nostrils. The great *Jos* & his attendants are also regaled with three cups brim-full of tea, which it is supposed are emptied by these tea drinking sociable Deities every night, & on the following morning are replenished by the Priest of the temple.

Whilst I was viewing this strange Pantheon, a resident recounted to me a curious anecdote respecting a Chinese mechanic. This man had frequently been engaged in Buonapartes service to make several ingenious pieces of furniture for him: amongst others he was ordered to fabricate a large cage, for the convenience & security of some of the General's birds. The cage was soon finished, & the Chinese thinking ingeniously to gratify the pride & ingratiate himself in the good opinion of his employer, carved with the utmost labour & care, a large wooden imperial eagle, & placed it soaring with outstretch'd wings on the top of the cage. This vile memento of past greatness

> "That brought to his remembrance from what state he fell,
> How glorious once"

thus palm'd upon him by an ignorant Chinese enraged Buonaparte to such a degree, that in a fury he dashed the eagle from his soaring position on the ground, greatly to the astonishment of the luckless fabricator, who from that time would never again work in the service of so choleric an employer, & one who so shamefully estimated the powers of his invention.

The day after our arrival I went to see Longwood. Upon entering the house inhabited by the once mighty Napoleon, one is apt to forget the lapse of time that has taken place since his death, & the present deserted state of the mansion & you begin to persuade yourself that his accommodations must have been wretched in the extreme.

NAPOLEON'S TOMB, ST. HELENA
"This wonderful man's last resting place"

The house which is small & inconsiderable, is now converted into farming premises: its situation is somewhat bleak & dreary, being upon a plain, scattered over with a grove of gum trees, the original wood of the island.

The apartment where the renowned Emperor breathed his last, is changed into a receptacle for a threshing machine, & the room in which his body was laid out in state, now serves as a stable for the convenience & comfort of four beautiful English cart-horses. If one felt inclined to moralize, how much might be here said on the instability of all human greatness.

The walls of the room in which he died, are pencilled over with various inscriptions in French & English, some moralizing on the wayward fate of the deceased hero, & others, here in bold letters giving the important communication that Mr. such a one visited Longwood, in the year so & so, & again there an elegant female running hand proclaims that such a young lady also arrived at this interesting spot in this or that year & day of the month. Many a scrap of French poetry laments the death of this chamber's once potent inhabitant.

We then went to the new house which is situated about one hundred yards from the old one. It is built in the handsomest style imaginable: no expense seems to have been spared, in rendering this place worthy of its intended illustrious occupier. The rooms which are all on a ground floor, are arranged in the most beautiful & elegant taste conceivable, & if the naked apartments thus strike you as magnificent, how different must have been the effect when supplied with the profusion of handsome furniture which once decorated them.

From this place we went to the tomb, which is removed about three quarters of a mile from Longwood. The road which is very good leads you along the margin of a dreary valley, called the "Devils Punch bowl", near which is situated the sequestered spot, chosen for this wonderful mans last resting place. On the ridge, looking down into the vale where his Tomb stands, is a neat cottage embosomed in fir trees, formerly occupied by Mad. Bertrand.

To this place Napoleon was wont to direct his evening walks, & having taken his coffee with the fair mistress of the little mansion, he generally accompanied her in a walk of a few hundred yards to the vale below, now the notorious spot in this most notorious island.

The walk brings you to a bright green fresh looking grass plot below. This is shaded by several weeping willows, & a beautifully clear transparent rill of water ensures a continual verdure, & heightens the beauty of this sequestered spot.

The trunk of one of these trees formed the Ex-Emperors accustomed seat, beneath which a tablet of two plain smooth stones, surrounded by an iron railing, now point out to the curious the narrow cell of its once all grasping inmate.

The natural beauty of the place is carefully preserved by a wooden railing placed round the tomb & willow trees, and a serjeant residing in a small house about 30 yards distant, takes care of the place & will allow you to enter the outer wooden Palisadoe, but you are not permitted to pass thro the iron railings without a written permit from the Governor himself. The soldier generally receives a Dollar from every visiter: he has made out a very touching story, which with many hard sounding words, & long misplaced epithets, he tells over and over again to each curious stranger, as the showman in Exeter [']change would recount the properties, & achievements of a mighty African Lion, or royal Bengal Tiger.

We found a youthful party from our Frigate amusing themselves here, some listening to the tales of the tedious dogmatical old soldier, & obtaining slips of willows for their Mama's & sisters, whilst others less sentimentally inclined, were seated on the tombstone, devouring bread & cheese & quaffing deep draughts of mellow beer, thus hoping I suppose to inhale in some degree a portion of the adventurous & daring spirit which once animated the mouldering frame beneath them.

What would a Frenchman have said to this impious profanation; they generally thoughtfully enter these (to them) sacred precincts, with a dejected air, reverently uncover their heads, muse a space, & then break forth in some passionate ejaculation.

I believe a sight of the tomb produces a very great emotion upon some of them.

One of my messmates during a moonlight contemplation at the

tomb was suddenly visited by the muses, and the following verses are the production of his poetic fancy.

Where weeping willows droop their head
  In silence and in gloom,
Their placid light the moon beams shed
  Upon a nameless tomb.

The Nig[h]tingale's sweet melody
  Is never warbled there,
And friendships votive flowers lie*
  Neglected on the bier.

Inscrib'd they nothing on the grave
  of him once deem'd a foe?
Left they nought there to tell the brave
  Napoleon sleeps below?

Nought here is heard of the trumpets thrill,
  War shout, or dying groan,
All, all is still, save yon trickling rill,
  Which murmurs near his stone.

Here could I stray, the summers day,
  And move with gentle tread,
Gaze on the ravage of decay,
Muse on the days that are pass'd away
  And the soon forgotten dead.

The remainder of the time we were here, I spent in visiting the different parts of the island: the roads are uncommonly good, and a stranger is gratified with scenery & views, in some parts of the most majestic description. That from Sandy Bay is beautiful beyond all power of expression. Most of the finest views have I understand been already taken; I therefore contented myself with three sketches only, one of Plantation house, one of Longwood, & the other of the Tomb.

We cannot but be all uncommonly pleased with our reception at this island. The Governor as I before said made us all in love with his character: at least ten or twelve of us were constantly at his house.

I forbear saying anything of the inhabitants of the place, the island having been already so much spoken of: we were however every where received with great Kindness and attention. We now prepared for our departure. We arrived on a Monday & proceeded immediately to the object of our visit, which was that of water & stock: the former we procured without any difficulty, hoses being conveyed into our boats from a stream running down to the sea from James's valley.

Stock however as well as everything else was uncommonly dear. On Saturday the 28th January we left this hospitable little island, and are now thank God, proceeding direct to England, having this day the 7th February once more crossed the equator.

* Mad: Bertrand planted herself various flowers at the foot, & head of his grave, which however have never flourished.

The journal of Robert Dampier ends here. During the first week of March the *Blonde* came across the wreck of the ship, the *Frances Mary*, with two women and four men still alive in the wreckage. After the rescue of the survivors, the *Blonde* continued on its homeward journey and anchored at Spithead on March 15, 1826.

THE RESCUE OF THE *FRANCES MARY*
"Her dismantled rigging indicated how severe had been her struggle with the elements"—BYRON, *Voyage*

NOTES

Page 3. H.M. FRIGATE BLONDE: The *Blonde*, a 46-gun frigate of the Royal Navy under the command of Lord Byron, left Portsmouth late in September 1824 to return the remains of Kamehameha II (Liholiho) and his queen Kamamalu to the Islands. Besides the complement of officers and men, the ship carried a surveyor, surgeon, artist and draftsman (Dampier), chaplain, naturalist, and botanist (see Introduction). Ralph S. Kuykendall, *The Hawaiian Kingdom, 1778–1854* (Honolulu, 1938), pp. 78–81; Great Britain, Public Record Office, *Journal of Proceedings of HMS* Blonde, *1824–1826*, microcopy (Honolulu, Hamilton Library).

Page 3. LORD BYRON: George Anson Byron became the seventh Baron Byron of Rochdale in 1824 upon the death of his first cousin, the poet. The account of the voyage published under his name included information from the diaries of various members of the expedition and was edited by Mrs. Maria Graham. Parts of that work were criticized as inaccurate (see Introduction). Lord Byron, *Voyage of HMS* Blonde *to the Sandwich Islands in the Years 1824–1825* (London, 1826). *An Examination of Charges Against the American Missionaries at the Sandwich Islands as Alleged in the Voyage of the Ship* Blonde, *and in the London Quarterly Review* (London, 1827). This pamphlet includes the discussion originally printed in the *North American Review* (Boston, January, 1828), and a few additional passages inserted for clarification. On Byron, see Cokayne's *The Complete Peerage*.

Page 3. KING AND QUEEN: Liholiho was the elder of the two sons of Kamehameha I and Keopuolani, his highest ranking wife. Born in 1797, Liholiho became king, with the title of Kamehameha II, upon the death of his father in 1819. Liholiho had five wives (see note p. 121), of whom Kamamalu was his favorite. The two traveled to England and died in London in the summer of 1824 (see Introduction). Samuel Kamakau, *Ruling Chiefs of Hawaii* (Honolulu, 1961), pp. 220 ff., 250 ff.

Page 3. SANDWICH ISLANDS: The Hawaiian Islands were discovered in 1778 by Capt. James Cook, who named them Sandwich Islands to honor the earl of Sandwich, then first lord of the Admiralty. J. C. Beaglehole, ed., *Journals of Captain James Cook* (Cambridge, 1967), III, pt. 1, 278. On John Montagu, fourth earl of Sandwich, see *Dictionary of National Biography*.

Page 3. THE SUITE: The original party left Hawaii November 27, 1823, on the English whaleship *L'Aigle* under the command of Capt. Valentine Starbuck (see note p. 126). Besides the king and queen, the party consisted of Boki, governor of Oahu, and his wife Liliha; chiefs Kapihe, Kekuanao'a, Manuia, and James Young Kanehoa; and the retainers Naukana, Ka'aiweuweu, and Kaulupaimalama (who died at sea on the voyage to England). John Rives, a Frenchman who resided in Hawaii, accompanied the party as interpreter but remained in England when the suite returned to Hawaii. Byron, *Voyage of HMS* Blonde, pp. 80–81; Kuykendall, *Hawaiian Kingdom*, pp. 76–81; Andrew Bloxam, *Diary* (Honolulu, 1925), p. 17.

Page 3. KOTESBUE: Lt. Otto von Kotzebue of the Russian Imperial Navy was in command of the *Rurick* [*Rurik*] in the summer of 1815 on an expedition of scientific exploration under the sponsorship of the chancellor of Russia. An English translation of his journal was published in 1821 and may have been seen by Dampier. Otto von Kotzebue, *A Voyage of Discovery, . . . 1815–1818* (London, 1821), p. 46; Peter H. Buck, *Explorers of the Pacific* (Honolulu, 1953), pp. 74–75.

Page 13. SMALL POX . . . HAZARD: Byron's concern for the health of the Hawaiians and fear of their susceptibility to such diseases as small pox was fully justified. The native population dropped from an estimated 300,000 in 1778 to about 31,000 in 1896. Diseases that reached epidemic proportions were the primary cause of depopulation among Hawaiians. An epidemic, perhaps of cholera, had already struck the Islands as early as 1803, and the small pox epidemic of 1853 was the worst experienced. Many sea captains were as conscientious as Byron, but some were indifferent to the fate of native populations. Robert C. Schmitt, *Demographic Statistics of Hawaii: 1778–1965* (Honolulu, 1968), pp. 41, 74.

Page 13. KAPIHE . . . DIED: Andrew Bloxam, naturalist aboard, described Kapihe as a Hawaiian who had absorbed much Western culture and showed great curiosity about mechanical devices. He spoke some English and sometimes served as interpreter for the Hawaiian party. He was said to have died as a result of "brain fever." James Macrae, botanist, listed Kapihe as admiral of the Sandwich Islands and stated that his death was from apoplexy. The Byron account recorded that Kapihe was "affected with an apparent determination of blood to the head" and died soon after. Bloxam, *Diary*, pp. 13–14; Byron, *Voyage of HMS* Blonde, p. 86; James Macrae, *With Lord Byron at the Sandwich Islands in 1825* (Honolulu, 1922), p. 4.

Page 15. FALL OF CALLAO: Dampier was a witness to the last resistance of Spanish forces to the armies of Simón Bolívar. The battle of Ayacucho in December 1824 resulted in the liberation of Peru and the success of the South American independence movement. The Spanish forces at Callao, however, refused to surrender the city to Bolívar and his patriot army and endured a two-year siege before capitulating. Dampier saw the beginning of the siege. Fredrick B. Pike, *The Modern History of Peru* (New York, 1967), p. 60.

Page 20. THE 4TH: This date does not agree with the rest of Dampier's chronology. Since "4th" is inserted above the line of writing, it may well have been entered later, or hastily, which would explain the inconsistency. The Byron (*Voyage of HMS* Blonde, p. 90) and Bloxam (*Diary*, p. 17) accounts state that the *Blonde* left Callao on the 17th. Macrae (*At the Sandwich Islands*, p. 4) gives the 16th. Thus, the 4th is certainly incorrect and the 17th appears to be the correct date.

Page 20. GALLAPAGOS: Discovered in 1535 by Tomás de Berlanga, bishop of Panama, the islands were named after the land tortoises found in profusion there. In the 1680s the islands began to be used as a rendezvous for English buccaneers sailing the Pacific between Callao and Panama to prey upon Spanish treasure ships. Among these visitors was William Dampier, successively buccaneer, circumnavigator, captain in the British Navy, and hydrographer. He was probably from the same family as the artist (see Introduction). When the *Blonde* stopped at the Galápagos, British and American fur traders and whalers were using the islands as a stopover on the long Pacific voyages. The fur traders also took the seals of the Galápagos. Victor W. Von Hagen, *Ecuador and the Galápagos Islands* (Norman, Okla., 1949), pp. 139 ff.

Page 21. ALBERMARLE ISLAND: The first general survey and chart of the islands of the Galápagos were made in 1684 by William Ambrose Cowley, the English buccaneer. Cowley named Albemarle after the first duke, George Monk. Spanish visitors called it Santa Isabel, and the official Ecuadorean name is Isabela. Islands were also named by the Spanish explorer, Capt. Don Alonso de Torres, in 1789, and the English naval officer, Capt. James Colnett, in 1793. After annexing the islands, Ecuador renamed the group Archipiélago de Colón in 1892 in honor of Columbus and also renamed the islands. These became the official names, but some maps indicate the English names in parentheses after the official ones. See, for instance, Reader's Digest, *Great World Atlas* (Pleasantville, N.Y., 1963), p. 92.

Page 21. BANK'S COVE: Banks' cove was named for Sir Joseph Banks, botanist on Cook's first voyage of exploration to the Pacific, 1768–1771 (see note on p. 123). Today, some localities, especially bays and coves, still bear their English names (see preceding note).

Page 21. NARBORO ISLAND: Narborough Island was named by Cowley after the Pacific navigator, Sir John Narborough. The island is now known as Fernandina.

Page 26. ABINGDON ISLAND: The English named the island after the earl of Abingdon; Ecuador calls it Pinta.

Page 26. ROBINSON CRUSOE LOOKING ISLANDS: Alexander Selkirk, a Scotsman, was a ship's master. After a disagreement with his captain, Selkirk was left on Juan Fernández Island for four years and four months. His experiences were probably the inspiration for Daniel Defoe's novel, *Robinson Crusoe*. Von Hagen, *Ecuador and the Galápagos Islands*, pp. 190 ff. See beginning of chapter 8 and note there.

Page 28. BOKI: Before an interview with George IV could be arranged, Liholiho died in London, and Boki became the head of the Hawaiian party and the spokesman for the Hawaiian government. Thus, it was Boki who was granted the interview with the king of England. The discussion centered around a proposal for the Hawaiian Islands to be recognized as a protectorate of England, which Kamehameha I was thought to have negotiated with Capt. George Vancouver of the Royal Navy in 1794. Boki stated that Kamehameha II had traveled to London to "confirm" this relationship. The Hawaiian party left England with the understanding that George IV had promised protection for the Islands from "evils from without." Boki and his wife Liliha were from Maui island families and of high rank. Boki was governor of Oahu in the 1820s and his elder brother, named variously Kalanimoku, Kalaimoku, Karaimoku, and Billy Pitt, was the chief minister of the Hawaiian Kingdom. Kamakau, *Ruling Chiefs*, pp. 256, 257, 287; John Ii, *Fragments of Hawaiian History* (Honolulu, 1959), pp. 53, 141, 159; *Polynesian*, October 18, 1851.

Page 28. AND HIS SUITE: The other accounts of the voyage include a description of the baptism as Christians of the Hawaiian party on May 1st. All except Boki were baptized and received the sacrament from the Reverend Richard Bloxam, chaplain of the *Blonde* and elder brother of the ship's naturalist, Andrew. The ceremony took place in the captain's cabin, and Lord Byron stood sponsor for the group. Boki had become a Christian in 1819 when he was baptized by the chaplain aboard *L'Uranie*, a French warship under the command of Capt. Louis de Freycinet. On board the *Blonde*, Boki had joined the ship's company in Easter services on April 3rd, and had then received the sacrament. Macrae, *At the Sandwich Islands*, p. 4; Bloxam, *Diary*, p. 19; Byron, *Voyage of HMS* Blonde, pp. 95–96.

Page 29. SOME LITTLE ANXIETY: Two whaling ships had brought word of the death of Kamehameha II to Hawaii on March 9, 1825, and the first British consul to the Hawaiian Kingdom, Capt. Richard Charlton, who landed in Honolulu in mid-April, reported the imminent arrival of the bodies of the royal couple. The observation that Boki and his party were uncertain, perhaps fearful, of their reception clarifies the Hawaiian political history of the era. By ancient Hawaiian tradition, upon the death of the highest chief, or king, political power descended to his named heir, who could drastically redistribute political place and land grants. Moreover, several factions of chiefs appear to have been close to Liholiho before his journey to England. Both these factors may have contributed to Boki's uneasiness. Kuykendall, *Hawaiian Kingdom*, pp. 71–74, 76–81, 118; Bloxam, *Diary*, p. 19.

Page 29. SPITHEAD: The roadstead for many ships leaving and returning to England.

Page 29. VANCOUVER: George Vancouver had first visited Hawaii when he served as a midshipman on Cook's third voyage to the Pacific, 1776–1780. He had previously been in the Pacific on Cook's second voyage, 1772–1775. In 1790 the Admiralty sent him in command of an expedition of exploration and diplomacy. He was to continue the survey not completed by Cook of the northwest American coast. He was instructed to undertake a diplomatic exchange between England and Spain in the Pacific Northwest and to winter in Hawaii and survey that area.

Vancouver visited the Hawaiian Islands in 1792, 1793, and 1794. He met the island kings and chiefs and witnessed their preparations for war. The islands were divided into three major kingdoms: Hawaii island; Maui, including Maui, Kahoolawe, Lanai, Molokai, and Oahu islands; and Kauai, including Kauai and Niihau. The control of the individual kings was being challenged by dissident chiefs at the same time that the kings were planning and conducting wars of conquest against each other. Thus, Vancouver saw the islands in the midst of the move toward the unification of all the islands under one king. This was accomplished by Kamehameha, the Hawaii island king, in 1810. Vancouver met and admired Kamehameha and wrote enthusiastically about him in dispatches and in his journal. The publication of Vancouver's journal contributed to Kamehameha's reputation in the Western world. Kuykendall, *Hawaiian Kingdom*, pp. 39–44; George Vancouver, *A Voyage of*

Discovery to the North Pacific Ocean and Round the World . . . in the "Discovery" (London, 1801), III, 203–205, 260–267.

Page 30. KARAIMOKU: Kalanimoku (see note on BOKI, p. 117), Boki's elder brother, was chief minister of the Kingdom. He served Kamehameha I and his sons in an office generally reminiscent of that of the British prime minister, and called himself Mr. Pitt or Billy Pitt when he learned that this was the name of his British counterpart. Kuykendall, *Hawaiian Kingdom*, p. 53.

Page 30. PRUSSIAN SAILOR [and] PILOT OF WELCH EXTRACTION: Bloxam (*Diary*, p. 21) stated that the Welshman's name was Davis. Macrae (*At the Sandwich Islands*, p. 5) described them as "two ragged white men."

Page 30. WAR [on] ATOOI: Even after Kamehameha I had united all eight islands, Kauai remained the most politically independent and was the only one Kamehameha never conquered in war. Instead, he entered into an agreement with the king, Kaumuali'i, in which Kauai became a tributary kingdom and Kaumuali'i a relatively independent island governor with Kamehameha as supreme political authority.

Kaumuali'i's submission remained incomplete. He was known to complain to Western traders about Kamehameha and to have sought an opportunity to regain independence. In 1815 this opportunity seemed to have arrived when Dr. George Scheffer came to the Islands. Sent by the Russian American Company of Alaska to investigate the possibility of establishing an agricultural colony in the Islands, the doctor exceeded his orders. He spent the next two years actively involved in political as well as agricultural activities. His objective was either to influence the Hawaiian government in favor of the Russian tsar or to seize the Islands in the tsar's name. Scheffer had his greatest success on Kauai and even convinced Kaumuali'i to sign a document placing his domain under Russian protection.

In 1819, on the death of Kamehameha I, Liholiho thought it necessary to travel to Kauai to make certain that Kaumuali'i acknowledged submission to the king of a united Hawaii. At the time of Dampier's visit, a new crisis had arisen. At the death of Kaumuali'i late in 1824, his son George attempted to reassert Kauai's independence and to revert to ancient political practices, in particular, the redistribution of land and the realignment of political power. Kamakau, *Ruling Chiefs*, pp. 187–195, 266–269; Klaus Mehnert, *The Russians in Hawaii: 1804–1819* (Honolulu, 1939), pp. 25 ff.

Page 30. FORT: Scheffer had built at least two forts on Kauai in 1816, at Hanalei and at Waimea where the Waimea River reached the sea. In the civil war of 1824 the Waimea fort was used by the forces of the Kingdom while a fort was erected by the insurgents at Wahiawa. Kamakau, *Ruling Chiefs*, pp. 267–268.

Page 33. KAHUMANU: Dampier's description later in the journal adds to our knowledge of one of the most important figures in Hawaiian history. Ka'ahumanu was the daughter of Ke'eaumoku one of the five Kona chiefs who supported Kamehameha I throughout his wars to conquer and unify the islands. She became one of Kamehameha's wives and his most loved companion. After his death in 1819, she became a powerful political figure and remained so until her own death in 1832.

Events in her life fill the narrative of Hawaiian history during that era. In the 1790s Ka'ahumanu and Kamehameha were estranged and finally reconciled as a result of the mediation of Vancouver. In 1819 she was one of the most effective of those who exerted pressure on Kamehameha II to break the ancient *kapu* system and to reject the ancient pagan religion. In the 1820s she at first treated the American missionaries with contempt, but by 1824 she was assisting them in their conversion and education programs by active political and financial support.

Ka'ahumanu's political power rested on her position as *kuhina nui*, a kind of super regent. She announced the position and title (both new) to Kamehameha II after his father's death, stating that the great Kamehameha had said on his deathbed that she was to share the rule with his son. Ii, *Fragments of Hawaiian History*, pp. 14, 53, 152; Kamakau, *Ruling Chiefs*, pp. 219–220; Vancouver, *Voyage of Discovery*, V, 10–11, 40–47; Kuykendall, *Hawaiian Kingdom*, pp. 63–64.

Page 34. MADAME BOKI'S FATHER: This was the chief Hoapili, one of the younger generation of counselors of Kamehameha I. He had been entrusted in 1819 with the sacred duty of finding a secret resting place for the bones of the great king. The fact that Kamehameha's tomb, probably in a cave, has not been found to date, indicates that Hoapili fulfilled his obligation well. Kamakau, *Ruling Chiefs*, p. 256; Kuykendall, *Hawaiian Kingdom*, pp. 53, 63.

Page 34. AMERICAN MISSIONARY: In 1820 a group of Protestant missionaries of the American Board of Commissioners for Foreign Missions arrived in Hawaii from Boston, Massachusetts, to bring Christianity and civilization to the Sandwich Islands. The Board represented an interdenominational group, primarily of Congregationalists and Presbyterians. Between 1820 and 1855 fifteen companies of American missionaries arrived. A company usually consisted of ordained ministers plus a staff of doctors, teachers, farmers, bookbinders, printers, and business agents. In all, more than three hundred Americans came to Hawaii during that period.

Dampier probably met the Reverend William Richards, a missionary who arrived in Hawaii in 1823, one of three ordained ministers in the third company. Richards settled at Lahaina, Maui, on May 31, 1823, and left the mission in 1838 to become an adviser to the Hawaiian monarch Kamehameha III. He served at various times as instructor in law and political economy, as diplomatic official for the Kingdom, and as minister of Public Instruction until his death in 1847. Rev. and Mrs. Orramel H. Gulick, *The Pilgrims of Hawaii* (New York, 1918), p. 341; Rufus Anderson, *History of the Sandwich Islands Mission* (Boston, 1870), pp. 235–236, 361; Hiram Bingham, *A Residence of Twenty-one Years in the Sandwich Islands* (New York, 1847), p. 262; *Missionary Album* (Honolulu, 1937), p. 153.

Page 35. COOK'S HEART: The report of the inadvertent maltreatment of Cook's body was apparently told to the *Blonde*'s chaplain, Bloxam, by the American missionary, Richards.

This story revives an old and discredited account of the funeral ritual which followed Cook's death. Because of its repetition here in Dampier's journal, it is necessary to examine the story in some detail. Several points need explication. It has been firmly established by anthropologists that cannibalism was not practiced in ancient Hawaii, nor was it knowingly part of the treatment of Cook's body, as Capt. Charles Clerke, second in command of the expedition, determined. After Cook's death on February 14, 1779, Clerke questioned many Hawaiians closely, repeatedly, and in a roundabout manner and was fully satisfied that Cook's body had not been subjected to such a practice.

The body was taken to a *heiau* or temple on top of the cliffs behind Kealakekua Bay. Such a *heiau* would have been *kapu* or restricted to all but the highest chiefs and the highest priesthood, especially during a burial ceremony.

The second point concerns the date of the story's first telling. Dampier's account of 1825 appears to be the earliest one written, though not published. A similar story was published in 1838 by the Reverend Sheldon Dibble, an American Protestant missionary, in his history: "The heart, liver, &c., of Captain Cook were stolen and eaten by some hungry children, who mistook them in the night for the inwards of a dog. The names of the children were Kupa, Mohoole, and Kaiwikoole. They are now aged men, and reside within a few miles of the station of Lahaina." His source was a printed history of Hawaii in the Hawaiian language, *Ka Mooolelo Hawaii*, and in 1843 James Jackson Jarves in his history (pp. 127–128) quoted directly from Dibble's translation of the Hawaiian work.

The final point concerns the authenticity of the story itself and the possible influence of American missionaries on its origins. The *Mooolelo* was the work of a group of eager young

Hawaiian students who quizzed their elders for source material. They asked a list of questions made up by the youths' missionary teachers. In recent years, scholars have pointed out inaccuracies in the work and questioned the methods and the results of the research.

Dibble's history and his translation of the *Mooolelo* have also been challenged in terms of their accuracy and objectivity. In 1931 John F. G. Stokes, historian and anthropologist, sought to prove that American missionaries were interested in besmirching the character of Cook in Hawaii and therefore repeated stories about him that were false or reinterpreted his actions to discredit him. In 1967 J. C. Beaglehole, editor of Cook's journals for the Hakluyt Society, also found Dibble inaccurate: "as some of Dibble's story is manifestly absurd, it is possible that he may be wrong here also [in identifying a man], and that the native 'authorities' from whom he derived his account rearranged the details after the event" (Beaglehole, ed., *Journals of Captain James Cook*, III, pt. 1, 556, n. 1).

The Reverend William Ellis, an English Protestant missionary, arrived in Hawaii in 1822 and remained two years. He first published his history in 1824. The American Protestant missionaries, the Reverend Charles Stewart, and the Reverend Hiram Bingham, each published their experiences of Hawaii, Stewart in 1828, Bingham in 1847. None of the three mentions the story told by Richards in 1825.

It is impossible to determine at this point the accuracy of the story or Richards' capacity for scholarly objectivity. Beaglehole, ed., *Journals of Captain James Cook*, III, pt. 1, 541 ff., 556 ff.; William Ellis, *Narrative of a Tour Through Hawaii or OWhyee*, 2nd ed. enl. (London, 1828); Bingham, *In the Sandwich Islands*; Sheldon Dibble, *History and General Views of the Sandwich Islands Mission* (Boston, 1843); John F. G. Stokes, "Origins of the Condemnation of Captain Cook in Hawaii," in *39th Annual Report* (for 1930) of the Hawaiian Historical Society. See notes, WITNESSED THE DEATH, p. 125, MORAI, p. 125, ACCUSTOMED FUNERAL RITE, p. 125.

Page 35. MR. CHARLTON: Capt. Richard Charlton was appointed the first British consul to the Sandwich, Society, and Friendly (Tonga) Islands in September 1824, in part as a result of the trip to England of Liholiho and the Hawaiian chiefs. Charlton met the *Blonde* on its outward voyage in early February at Valparaiso, Chile, and was in Honolulu to meet Byron in May.

Later Charlton became embroiled with the Hawaiian government in a bitter controversy over land. In 1843 Lord George Paulet of the British Navy sailed H.M.S. *Carysfort* into Honolulu harbor and proceeded to make demands on the Hawaiian government in favor of the interests of British subjects. One of the issues concerned Charlton's land claims. Kamehameha III refused to accede to Paulet's demands and as an alternative surrendered, under protest, his authority to that of Great Britain. Paulet's actions and the cession of the Islands were repudiated by the British government. In 1825 Charlton was not in conflict with the Hawaiian government. Byron, *Voyage of HMS* Blonde, pp. 85–86; Bloxam, *Diary*, pp. 13–14; Kuykendall, *Hawaiian Kingdom*, p. 80; Montague Paske-Smith, *Early British Consuls in Hawaii* (Honolulu, 1936), pp. 3–5.

Page 35. A FORT FROM THE TOWN [and] ONE ON THE HEIGHTS: A fort had been built during Kamehameha I's time at Honolulu harbor. The ground plan had been laid out by Dr. George Scheffer in 1816. The uncompleted fort was finished by one of Kamehameha's chiefs, perhaps John Young. The volcanic crater behind Honolulu was also fortified. This was called Kekuanohu by the Hawaiians and Punchbowl by Westerners. Kamakau, *Ruling Chiefs*, p. 273; Kuykendall, *Hawaiian Kingdom*, pp. 57–58; Mehnert, *Russians in Hawaii*, pp. 22–35.

Page 35. LITTLE KING: Kauikeaouli, born 1813, was then eleven years of age, the second son of Keopuolani and Kamehameha I. He became Kamehameha III after news of his brother's death reached Hawaii in 1825, and he ruled until his death in late 1854. During his reign he saw a traditional Polynesian culture become more and more influenced by alien Western values. Kauikeaouli was modern enough to accept change and yet traditional enough to regret much of that change. Dampier saw him at his happiest. Kamakau, *Ruling Chiefs*, pp. 259, 260, 263.

Page 35. CHURCH ESTABLISHED HERE: In 1820 Protestant missionaries established a church at Honolulu under the guidance of Bingham. The building is described by Gulick as "a very large thatched building . . . erected . . . upon the grounds of the present Kawaiaha'o Cemetery." A coral stone building was later built there. Gulick, *Pilgrims of Hawaii*, p. 26; Bingham, *In the Sandwich Islands*, p. 215.

Page 36. DISCONSOLATE WIDOW: Polygamy and polyandry were part of ancient Hawaiian practice, especially among the chiefs and chiefesses. Liholiho's five wives were (see note KING AND QUEEN, p. 115): Kamamalu, Kekauluohi, Kalanipauahi, Kekau'onohi, and Kina'u. It is not clear to which wife the text refers, perhaps it is Kina'u. Kamakau, *Ruling Chiefs*, p. 250.

Page 37. TWO AMERICAN MISSIONARIES: Bingham was one of the two ordained ministers in the first company of American missionaries. He headed the Honolulu mission station until his departure in 1840 and was very influential in all Hawaiian affairs. Stewart was also at Honolulu in 1825. Levi Chamberlain, business agent, and Elisha Loomis, printer, were at Honolulu, but the first two were the only ministers proper. Stewart, *Residence in the Sandwich Islands*, pp. 339–340; Bingham, *In the Sandwich Islands*, p. 263.

Page 37. MARINI: Francisco de Paula Marin, a Spaniard, arrived in the Islands about 1794 and remained until his death in 1837. Macrae, *At the Sandwich Islands*, pp. 15, n. 18, 68-70; Kuykendall, *Hawaiian Kingdom*, pp. 53, 68. A short account of Marin's life is given in Antoinette Withington, *The Golden Cloak* (Honolulu, 1953), pp. 96–110.

Page 38. PATCHES OF STAGNANT WATER: Wet taro planting involved the clearing and leveling of an area and the forming of earth banks. Water was let into the patch and, although slow moving, it did not become stagnant. Edwin H. Bryan, Jr., *Ancient Hawaiian Life* (Honolulu, 1938), p. 12; Peter H. Buck, *Arts and Crafts of Hawaii* (Honolulu, 1964), p. 10; Alonzo Chapin, "Remarks on the Sandwich Islands: their Situation, Climate, Diseases, and their suitableness as a resort for individuals affected with or predisposed to Pulmonary Disease," *Hawaiian Spectator*, July, 1838.

Page 38. THE SANDWICH COLORS: The exact origin of the Hawaiian flag is still in dispute, and there is an extensive bibliography on the subject. It is known that at the suggestion of one of his advisers, perhaps Capt. Alexander Adams or Capt. George Beckley, Kamehameha I had his own flag designed with a series of horizontal red, white, and blue stripes and a British Union Jack in the upper left-hand corner. The combination was supposed to represent American and British influence in Hawaii. It had been Kamehameha's practice to raise the flag of the nation whose ship was then in port. When ships of several nations appeared at the same time, to avoid ill feelings, a Hawaiian flag was created. American and British ships were the most numerous in Hawaiian ports and the people of the two nations the most important to Hawaii.

It is not known whether the first flag had seven or eight stripes, whether the stripes began from the top with blue, white, or red, and what sequence the colors followed. The flag was probably first raised in 1816 and was not permanently lowered as the flag of an independent nation until 1898 when Hawaii was annexed to the United States. It is now the flag of the state of Hawaii. Edith B. Williams, *Ka Hae Hawaii, The Story of the Hawaiian Flag* (Honolulu, ca. 1963); Victor Houston, *Hawaiian Flag* (Honolulu, 1954); W. D. Alexander, "The Maker of the Hawaiian Flag," in *6th Annual Report* (for 1898) of the Hawaiian Historical Society.

Page 42. MAITAI: The word *maika'i* in Hawaiian denotes approbation in the sense of good, excellent, and also handsome. Mary Kawena Pukui and Samuel H. Elbert, *Hawaiian-English Dictionary* (Honolulu, 1965).

Page 43. PORTRAITS: The portraits of Kauikeaouli and Nahi'ena'ena were presented to the Honolulu Academy of Arts in 1951 by

Mrs. C. Montague Cooke, Jr., Mrs. Heaton Wrenn, and Charles M. Cooke, III, in memory of Dr. C. Montague Cooke, Jr. Photographic reproductions of the paintings are included in this edition on pages 44, 45.

Page 44. CUTANEOUS DISORDER: Dampier was describing "an infestation with the scabies mite, *Sarcoptes scabei.*" Private note from Dr. O. A. Bushnell, University of Hawaii.

Page 47. STONE AXE . . . ENGLISH ADZE: The primary tool of the Hawaiians and Polynesians was a stone adze. When metal was introduced the Hawaiians began replacing the stone head with an iron one. Thus, the tool would have been more accurately described as a "stone adze transformed into an English adze." David Malo, *Hawaiian Antiquities* (Honolulu, 1903), pp. 76–78; E. S. Craighill Handy et al., *Ancient Hawaiian Civilization* (Honolulu, 1933), pp. 124–125, 226–227; Bryan, *Ancient Hawaiian Life*, pp. 37–38.

Page 47. BARK OF THIS TREE: It is not clear whether Dampier is referring to the breadfruit or the coconut tree. Hawaiians made an inferior tapa out of the bark of the breadfruit, *Artocarpus incisa*, but the bark of the coconut, *Cocos nucifera*, was not used for cloth. The best tapa was made from the bark of the paper mulberry, *Broussonetia papyrifera*. Buck, *Arts and Crafts*, p. 168.

Page 48. KARAIMOKU . . . CURE: Kalaimoku still maintained his place as the chief minister of the Kingdom until his death in February 1827.

Page 49. SELECTED A BOY & A GIRL: The portraits of these two young people, done in oil by Dampier, were left to the governor of the Sandwich Islands in the will of F. E. C. Byron, 10th Baron and ordained minister, together with two oil paintings of the *Blonde* at sea. Byron died in 1949, and the paintings arrived in Hawaii in 1952. All four now hang in Washington Place, Honolulu, the official residence of the governor of Hawaii. Correspondence, Archives of Hawaii. Photographic reproductions of the portraits may be found on pages 48, 49 and of the seascapes on pages 105 and 113.

Page 49. CHIEFS . . . ANOTHER RACE: The comment was frequently made by the foreign resident in Hawaii and the casual visitor that the difference between the chiefs and the common folk was discernible in physical appearance as well as in social structure. Stature, size, features, skin color, and the like were often noted as marking a distinction in class. And some thought this was probably a result of inbreeding, the extra care and nurture which came with wealth, and the assurance that accompanied the rank of chief. Beaglehole, ed., *Journals of Captain James Cook*; Ellis, *Tour Through Hawaii*; Bingham, *In the Sandwich Islands*; Stewart, *Residence in the Sandwich Islands.*

Page 50. BOKI: The chief now so admired by Dampier did not become the dominant political figure in Hawaii. When his brother Kalaimoku died in early 1827, Boki was already at odds with his society. He had antagonized the two most powerful groups in the Islands: Ka'ahumanu and the majority of chiefs who supported her, and the American Protestant missionaries. Boki was close to the young king Kauikeaouli and attempted to influence the king's behavior and his political decisions. Primarily in reaction to Ka'ahumanu and the Puritans, perhaps partly because of the circumstances of his own conversion to Christianity, Boki supported the Catholic Church mission in Hawaii and plotted to seize political power by warfare if necessary. He tried several commercial ventures, none of which proved profitable. In 1829, in debt and with his political influence in decline, Boki took two ships and more than four hundred men on an expedition to the New Hebrides in search of sandalwood. He apparently also intended to settle a colony at Erromanga in that group. Six months after he left Hawaii, news arrived that he had been lost at sea, probably sailing between Rotuma and Erromanga The second ship, with twenty men, returned to Hawaii. Kamakau, *Ruling Chiefs*, pp. 270–296; Ii, *Hawaiian History*, pp. 154–157; Bingham, *In the Sandwich Islands*, pp. 305, 339–364; Gavan Daws, "The High Chief Boki: A Biographical Study in Early Nineteenth Century Hawaiian History," *Journal of the Polynesian Society*, March, 1966.

Page 50. MEETING OF THE CHIEFS: The meeting was held on June 6, 1825, and included all the high chiefs, Byron, Charlton, two missionaries (probably Bingham and Stewart), several American merchants, and a few of the *Blonde*'s complement. It was one of the most important political events of the period. Kauikeaouli's succession to the title as Kamehameha III was confirmed. The chiefs also decided that Kalanimoku was to be given guardianship of the king, the American missionaries were to be his instructors, and land titles were to remain in the ownership of the present holders. Criminal and constitutional laws were discussed. Boki made an eloquent speech as did Lord Byron. Byron had been provided with secret instructions by the foreign office authorizing him to declare the Islands under British protection or to claim them as a British possession if he thought that the situation warranted such action (see Introduction). The chiefs appeared to be divided in their support of English or American power. Boki had returned from England an ardent admirer of the English. Ka'ahumanu and other chiefs seemed more interested in increasing the influence of American merchants and missionaries.

None of this political tension appears in Dampier's account. Bloxam, *Diary*, p. 48; Macrae, *At the Sandwich Islands*, p. 43; Byron, *Voyage of HMS* Blonde, pp. 152–157; Kamakau, *Ruling Chiefs*, pp. 273–274; Kuykendall, *Hawaiian Kingdom*, pp. 119–120; Bingham, *In the Sandwich Islands*, pp. 264–270; Great Britain, Foreign Office, "Secret Instructions to Lord Byron, September 14, 1824," in *Report for the Two Years Ending December 31, 1926* of the Historical Commission of the Territory of Hawaii (Honolulu, 1927).

Page 51. THROWING A CIRCULAR STONE: The Hawaiians had a form of bowling which involved throwing a shaped stone. Stone and game were called 'ulu maika.' Bucks, *Arts and Crafts*, pp. 372–373.

Page 53. FRESH WATER STREAM: Hilo Bay was also called Waiakea Bay. At least two freshwater streams emptied into the bay: the Wailuku and the Waiakea. The headwaters of the Wailuku were at the top of Mauna Kea, and the stream was characterized by rapids and waterfalls. The Waiakea was a quiet stream, navigable by ships of relatively large size. Ellis, *Tour Through Hawaii*, pp. 286–353; Byron, *Voyage of HMS* Blonde, pp. 164–167, 254; Bloxam, *Diary*, p. 51.

Page 54. TWO MISSIONARIES . . . STATIONED HERE: Joseph Goodrich, a licensed preacher, and Samuel Ruggles, a teacher, were stationed in Hilo in 1825. Goodrich had been instrumental in the conversion of the female chief Kapi'olani (see also note, p. 123). *Missionary Album*, pp. 16, 93, 159.

Page 54. BYRON . . . TO LIVE ON SHORE: Byron's house was situated on the banks of the Wailuku River. Byron, *Voyage of HMS* Blonde, pp. 164–167.

Page 54. SIR JOSEPH BANKS: Banks (1743–1820) was the naturalist aboard Cook's first expedition to the Pacific from 1768 to 1771. Educated at Harrow, Eton, and Christ Church, Oxford, Banks was the *bon vivant* of that voyage. Handsome, wealthy, and sophisticated, he was a favorite among the female chiefs of Tahiti and an admirer of Tahitian beauty. He was created a baronet in 1781. *Dictionary of National Biography*.

Page 54. MR. RUGGLES AND KAHUMANU: As already stated (see note, p. 118), Ka'ahumanu was beginning to change her attitude toward Christianity and the missionaries between 1824 and 1825.

Page 57. WATERFALL: In the Wailuku River.

Page 57. PALEY VOLCANO: Dampier apparently meant Pele, goddess of fire, who lived in volcanoes. Her home was, and is, considered to be in Kilauea Crater on the slope of Mauna Loa where the volcanic activity testified to her presence. Bryan, *Ancient Hawaiian Life*, p. 61; Malo, *Hawaiian Antiquities*, p. 113.

Page 58. TEA TREE: Dampier confused the ti plant with the candlenut or *kukui* tree, *Aleurites moluccana*. The broad leaves of the ti plant were used in cooking, wrapping, clothing, etc. The nut of the *kukui*, rich in oil, was baked and the whole nut strung on a coconut leaf rib to make a candle. A ti plant rarely grew to tree proportions, while a *kukui* tree was usually tall and broad in size. Malo, *Hawaiian Antiquities*, p. 42; Buck, *Arts and Crafts*, p. 107.

Page 61. YACAUN: Apparently Dampier's spelling of Waiakea, a name for Hilo Bay.

Page 61. KAOPELLANI: The female chief Kapi'olani became a devout Christian and a supporter of the American Protestant mission.

In late 1824 she sought to destroy belief in the ancient gods, and to this end she walked to Kilauea Crater, descended into the pit, and there defied the ancient goddess of fire and volcanoes, Pele. "Jehovah is my God," she said. "He kindled these fires. I fear not Pele . . . if I trust in Jehovah . . . he shall save me from the wrath of Pele. . . ." No harm came to Kapi'olani at that time.

This incident is said to have helped greatly in breaking the hold that idolatry still had on Hawaii. Kapi'olani was the wife of the chief Naihe, and both were powerful chiefs with extensive land holdings and political power. Later Kapi'olani suffered with cancer and in 1841 died in excruciating pain but with seeming calmness of spirit. Bingham, *In the Sandwich Islands*, pp. 254, 257.

Page 63. BYRON'S BAY: As Dampier noted, Hilo or Waiakea Bay had not been entered before by a ship as large as the *Blonde*. Ka'ahumanu dedicated the area to Byron and ordered that henceforth the bay would be known only by his name. Runners were sent out to inform the Hawaiians of her edict. Byron, *Voyage of HMS* Blonde, pp. 164–167, 254; Bloxam, *Diary*, p. 51.

Page 63. KING'S PILOT, AN ENGLISHMAN: This was Capt. Alexander Adams, a former sea captain who had been in the service of Kamehameha I in 1816 and who may have suggested the design of the Hawaiian flag (see note, p. 121).

Page 63. MUTINY: In April 1825 the *Asia*, a Spanish line-of-battle ship of seventy-four guns, appeared in Monterey harbor flying the flag of the United States. The ship was in the control of partisans of Latin American independence. Previously, the *Asia* had been part of the royal Spanish squadron operating against patriot forces along the coast of South America. After it became apparent that the Spanish had been defeated in Peru and Chile in January 1824, the ship was ordered to sail for Manila in the Philippines. In the Mariana Islands a revolt occurred in March 1825, and the ship was seized by the officers and men who were sympathetic to the independence movement. Commanded by José Martínez, the *Asia* returned east to Monterey to surrender to the American enemies of Spain. The men swore allegiance to independence and the federal constitution of Mexico, and the *Asia* joined the Mexican navy. Whether the ship and its crew had engaged in acts of piracy or had burnt a ship of the United States upon the high seas cannot be confirmed. Hubert Howe Bancroft, *History of California 1825–1840*, pp. 24–27, in *Works*, vol. 20 (San Francisco, 1885).

Page 64. KARAKAKOOA: Kealakekua Bay, Kona, Hawaii, lies in a northwest to southwest curve on the west coast of the island of Hawaii. The arc of the beach is backed by steep cliffs at the curve's center. This is the area visited by Cook from January 17 until his death. To the north and west was the village of Ka'awaloa: there, on February 14, 1779, Cook was killed. At about the center of the beach's curve was the *heiau* of Hikiau and its surrounding sweet potato fields where Cook erected his observatories to view the stars and carry out other scientific experiments. Just above the *heiau* was the pond and watering place where Cook got fresh water; just below the *heiau* was the village of Kakooa. Beaglehole, ed., *Journals of Captain James Cook*, III, pt. 2, 1175.

Page 65. KAYROOA WHERE COOK WAS KILLED: See preceding note. The village Dampier referred to was probably Kakooa, now named Napo'opo'o. Other villages in the area were Kealakekua, Waipunaula, Kalama, and Kahauloa. About sixteen miles north along the Kona coast is Kailua, then often pronounced *Kairua* and spelled *Kayrooa*. Kayrooa may be Dampier's spelling of either Ka'awaloa or of Kakooa. The sketch on p. 66 is most probably of Kealakekua Bay; the original bears the title "Kairua Bay." Beaglehole, ed., *Journals of Captain James Cook*, III, pt. 1, 268, 531–561; pt. 2, 1175–1176.

Page 65. MORAI WHERE COOK FIXED HIS OBSERVATORY: Cook's observatories and tents were set up on the *heiau* called Hikiau soon after his arrival on January 17, 1779, and again on February 11, after Cook's ships had left and then returned to Kealakekua Bay. The *heiau* was always *kapu* to the people. The local priests put a *kapu* on the surrounding area also to preserve Cook's equipment from the curious intruder and the filcher. Beaglehole, ed., *Journals of Captain James Cook*, III, pt. 1, cxiv, cxlvii, 268, 491, 505–507; pt. 2, 1191.

Page 65. NAHI: Naihe, sometimes Nahe, was the son of a Hawaiian chief from Kona named Keaweaheulu. The latter was one of the original five Kona chiefs who encouraged Kamehameha to seek the conquest of the islands, and he remained one of the kingdom's most important counselors. At his death Naihe succeeded his father and served Kamehameha I, II, and III in important positions. Ii, *Hawaiian History*, pp. 81, 83, 117, 153; Kuykendall, *Hawaiian Kingdom*, p. 53.

Page 65. WITNESSED . . . THE DEATH: Naihe's report generally substantiates other accounts of Cook's death but does not include the tale that Richards told Bloxam. It is evident from his comments that the Hawaiians admired and venerated Cook in 1779 and continued to hold his memory in deep respect in 1825. Beaglehole, ed., *Journals of Captain James Cook*, III, pt. 1, lxxi, lxxv, 531–562.

Page 67. MORAI . . . WHERE COOK'S BODY WAS CUT UP: This *heiau* was situated inland, on top of the cliffs fronting the bay. During the altercation on February 14, 1779, Cook and several marines were killed by the Hawaiians. Those of Cook's men who remained aboard ship watched through their glasses and saw the Hawaiians take the bodies "over a Hill up the Country." The *heiau* was called Kupuhiolono after Cook's death. The name meant "the place of the burning of Lono [Cook]." It may have been the area that the Hawaiians called Maunaloia. Beaglehole, ed., *Journals of Captain James Cook*, III, pt. 1, 540, 541, n. 4, 547, 555 ff., 566 ff.; Macrae, *At the Sandwich Islands*, p. 70; Bloxam, *Diary*, p. 77; Kamakau, *Ruling Chiefs*, p. 103.

Page 67. ACCUSTOMED FUNERAL RITE: Cook's body was treated with the respect and ceremony given the highest chief. Thus, though the stranger might find these funeral practices horrifying, the Hawaiians were giving due honor and respect to a man they had admired, loved, and worshipped. Beaglehole, ed., *Journals of Captain James Cook*, III, pt. 1, clviii, 542, n. 4; Malo, *Hawaiian Antiquities*, pp. 131–135.

Page 67. GOVERNOR JOHN ADAMS OR COQUINI: The chief Kuakini was the brother of Ka'ahumanu and son of Ke'eaumoku. His American bias, obvious in his choice of name, was shown in his speeches before the councils of chiefs, and in his antagonism to Boki and Liliha. When Boki left for the New Hebrides in 1829, Liliha was given the "care" of King Kauikeaouli and also made governor of Oahu. She was accused by Ka'ahumanu, many chiefs, and the American missionaries of living a dissolute life and of influencing the king to emulate her. In October 1830, a council of chiefs deposed her and gave the governorship of Oahu to Kuakini who already had positions of power. He introduced a puritanical regime, issuing edicts on keeping the Sabbath and against the sale of liquor, adultery, and the like.

Kuakini was apparently more rigid in his choice of edicts than in his behavior. Chased by an irate husband, it was said, he jumped over a wall and broke the bones in his foot. He became permanently lame and "thereafter, when he fought with his wife and she ran away from him he could not pursue her because of his lameness." Ii, *Hawaiian History*, pp. 53, 81, 101, 166, 169; Kuykendall, *Hawaiian Kingdom*, pp. 125, 130–132; Kamakau, *Ruling Chiefs*, pp. 297–305.

Page 67. A CELEBRATED MORAI: The *heiau* at Honaunau was of a special type apparently unique to Hawaii. It was a *pu'uhonua* or *heiau* of refuge for the guilty fugitive, the noncombatant in war, and even the defeated soldier. Sanctuary was given to those who reached the temple precincts until they were cleared of guilt or safe from war. A charnel house at Honaunau named *Hale o Keawe* was a sacred depository for the bones of departed kings and chiefs. Ellis, *Tour Through Hawaii*, pp. 152–157.

Page 67. NO WHITE MAN BEFORE OUR ARRIVAL: Ellis traveled around the island of Hawaii in 1822, visited Honaunau, and saw and described *Hale o Keawe*, but he was not allowed to enter the temple. Ellis, *Tour Through Hawaii*, pp. 152–158.

Page 67. RAPACIOUS INCLINATIONS: Many of the images and souvenirs collected by the *Blonde*'s men have appeared in museum collections in England and Hawaii.

Page 70. ERECT A SORT OF MONUMENT: The monument was placed at the *heiau* of Kapuhiolono (see note MORAI, p. 125). In 1850 the Byron monument was still erect, as reported in a Honolulu newspaper, but by 1876 the plaque was no longer in evidence.

In that year a more elaborate cenotaph was erected at Kaʻawaloa. The money to build it had been collected by subscription in Hawaii, and the land upon which it was constructed was made available by the Princess Miriam Likelike, governor of Hawaii island. *The Friend*, January 4, 1850. pp. 2–3; *Hawaiian Directory, 1880–1881*, pp. 552–553.

Page 70. A BETTER ANCHORAGE: Cook had worked along the west coast of Hawaii for some twelve days before discovering Kealakekua Bay. During those days, Lt. William Bligh would take soundings along the shore and on January 16, 1779, he returned from such a trip with the news that he had found a safe harbor. In March Cook left and returned to Kealakekua, again indicating that he trusted the anchorage at Kealakekua. Beaglehole, ed., *Journals of Captain James Cook*, III, pt. 1, 503.

Page 73. STARBUCKS ISLAND: Dampier describes the confusion experienced over the islands observed. Byron thought that the first island seen was Starbuck and, later, that Watteoo or Atiu in the Herveys was visited. Actually the *Blonde* stopped first at an island that proved to be a new discovery and was then named Malden by Byron. The ship then sailed by an island that proved to be Starbuck. Finally, she stopped at Mauti or Mauke in the Cook Islands (not Atiu in the Herveys) and then turned east to the coast of South America. William T. Brigham, *An Index to the Islands of the Pacific Ocean* (Honolulu, 1900), pp. 47, 129, 149; Bloxam, *Diary*, pp. 79–91; Byron, *Voyage of HMS* Blonde, pp. 204–208; Macrae, *At the Sandwich Islands*, pp. 74–75.

Page 74. SEVERAL SQUARES: Dampier did a sketch of the rock formations although he did not land on the island. Anthropologists believe the traces of human habitation to have been left by Polynesians.

Page 74. COOK LIKEWISE MENTIONS: Perhaps Dampier is suggesting that Cook stopped at this island, but it does not appear that he did. The *Blonde*'s stop was apparently the first European visit.

Page 74. MALDEN'S ISLAND: The island did prove to be a new discovery and is still identified as Malden Island.

Page 74. STARBUCK . . . HIS ISLAND: Capt. Valentine Starbuck discovered the island that bore his name. It was also known as Volunteer. Starbuck was captain of the *L'Aigle* (see note THE SUITE, p. 115). Brigham, *Islands of the Pacific*, p. 149.

Page 74. WATTEOO: This name was given by Cook to Atiu in the Hervey group which he discovered in 1777. The island the *Blonde* visited proved to be Mauke (called Mauti by Cook) in the Cook Island group (see note STARBUCK ISLAND, above).

Page 75. MEMBER OF THE LONDON MISSIONARY SOCIETY: In March 1797, members of the London Missionary Society landed in Tahiti. It was not long before native teachers were trained in Christian fundamentals and sent to neighboring Pacific islands to prepare the way for conversion. The two teachers described by Dampier were Haavi and Faraire. Haavi was originally from Raiatea in the Society Islands, and Faraire was also probably from the Societies. In October 1825 Robert Bourne (see note below) revisited the island and found that the whole population of about two hundred had embraced Christianity, but that literacy had not progressed greatly because the books were in the Tahitian language and not the native dialect. C. W. Newbury, ed., *The History of the Tahitian Mission 1799–1830* (London, 1961), pp. 322–323; London Missionary Society, *Narrative of the Mission at O taheite and Other Islands in the South Seas . . .* (London, 1818), frontispiece.

Page 78. PARRY'S ISLAND: The island was named by Lord Byron in honor of Capt. William Edward Parry who had been in the Arctic seas in 1818 and 1819 in search of a northwest passage. Parry did not become the official name and the island continued to be called Mauke. On Parry, see *Dictionary of National Biography*.

Page 78. MR. WILLIAMS & MR. BOURNE: John Williams and Bourne sailed from England in the fall of 1816 to join the London Missionary Society in Tahiti. Williams was active in extending missionary work beyond the Society Islands and was killed in Erromanga in 1839 on such a mission. James Hutton, *Missionary Life in the Southern Seas* (London, 1874), pp. 280–282.

Page 79. ROBINSON CRUSOE: Selkirk lived for four years and four months on Juan Fernández (see chapter 2, p. 26, and note, p. 116).

Page 79. CAMBRIDGE, BRITON . . .: The vessels were all ships of the Royal Navy.

Page 82. STATE'S MORE INVETERATE ENEMIES THE INDIANS: The Araucanian Indian tribes were the largest Indian group to preserve their identity in southwestern America. They were never subdued by the Spanish but in the late eighteenth century agreed to live in peace with the European settlers. Since they periodically reverted to war against the Spanish, the colonial governments pursued a policy of pacification, holding meetings called parliaments. On these occasions, beside the formal talks, elaborate festivities were held. During the war for Chilean independence, the Araucanians were as often supporters of the royalists as they were of the patriots. One important leader who consistently favored the patriots was the chief Venancio, who fought with Bernardo O'Higgins in his campaigns. Stephen Clissold, *Bernardo O'Higgins and the Independence of Chile* (New York, 1969), pp. 17–27, 215–216; Simon Collier, *Ideas and Politics of Chilean Independence* (Cambridge, 1967), pp. 27–28, 212–217.

Page 83. CAPTAIN HALL: Capt. Basil Hall visited the Pacific Coast of South America in the early 1820s and later wrote of his experiences. *Extracts from a journal written on the coasts of Chile, Peru, and Mexico, in the years 1820, 1821, 1822* (Edinburgh, 1824).

Page 86. GENERAL FREIRE: Ramón Freire Serrano (1787–1851) was one of the noted patriots of Chile. The war for independence against Spain began in 1810 and lasted until about 1818. By that date Chile was considered free of Spanish control except for small areas of resistance such as at Callao and on Chiloe Island. While independence was gained, Chile did not achieve political stability for another decade. The patriots fought among themselves and the period 1817–1830 was an era of political turbulence and dictatorship. Bernardo O'Higgins was dictator until 1823 when he was compelled to resign by his former compatriots. Freire succeeded him as dictator and remained the political leader until about 1827. Luis Galdames, *History of Chile*, translated by Isaac J. Cox (New York, 1964), pp. 205 ff.

Page 88. CHILEAN ADMIRAL'S WIFE: The Admiral, Manuel Blanco Encalada, joined the Chilean revolutionists in 1813, organized the navy, and served briefly as president ad interim in 1826.

Page 88. MRS. GRAHAM'S HISTORY: Maria Graham, afterwards Lady Callcott, wrote the *Journal of a residence in Chile, during the year 1822, and a voyage from Chile to Brazil in 1823* (London, 1824). She was first married to Capt. Thomas Graham of the Royal Navy. Widowed in 1822, Mrs. Graham lived in Valparaiso for several months and traveled extensively in the vicinity. Upon her return to England, she married the artist, Augustus Wall Callcott, who was knighted in 1837. Mrs. Graham was a noted author and was editor of the Byron account of the voyage of the *Blonde*. British Museum, *Catalogue of Printed Books*; *Dictionary of National Biography*.

Page 90. MARQUIS OF LAREINE: Perhaps this was Juan Enríque Rosales Fuentes who was connected with the Chilean aristocracy through his mother and his wife. The latter was a member of the Larrain clan, and her husband was elected a member of the colonial aristocracy in 1808. Galdames, *History of Chile*, pp. 205 ff.

Page 92. LEREYNES: Same as Lareine, Larrain?

Page 97. A LARGE FRENCH FORCE: Rear Admiral de Rosamel, Claude-Charles Marie Ducampe, commanded a French naval mission in 1823 which was ordered to remain in South American waters and to visit and observe the new nations of Brazil, Chile, and Peru. Jean Paul Faivre, *L'Expansion française dans le Pacifique 1800–1842* (Paris, 1953), pp. 315–323.

Page 97. CARRERA: José Miguel Carrera was the first president of Chile. His two brothers were killed in the wars of independence. By 1825 the Carreras were at odds with their former compatriots. Galdames, *History of Chile*; Clissold, *Bernardo O'Higgins*.

Page 100. DR. ROBERTSON: William Robertson (1721–1793), principal of the University of Edinburgh, wrote the *History of America*

(London, 1777) in two volumes. In his biography in the 19th edition (1812, p. 67) it was stated that Robertson perceiving "that a History of America, confined solely to the operations and concerns of the Spaniards, would not be likely to excite a very general interest, he resolved to include in his plan the transaction of all European nations in the New World."

Page 104. TEMPESTUOUS EUROCLYDON [and] VIDE NOTE IN MANT'S BIBLE: The quote from Acts is: "But not long after there arose against it a tempestuous wind, called Euroclydon."

Page 104. LA ROCHEIN: Anthony La Roché reported the discovery of an island in 1675 in the South Atlantic which he named Isla Grande. It was thought to be located at about latitude 45°S and longitude 48°W. Ships sailing the area in the eighteenth and nineteenth centuries failed to find the island again. Vincent T. Harlow, *The Founding of the Second British Empire, 1763–1793* (London, 1952), I, 47, 125–126, 131–132.

Page 104. NAPOLEON'S FEELINGS: Napoleon was transferred from the *Bellerophon* to the *Northumberland* and arrived at St. Helena in mid-October 1815. Descriptions of the island confirm that the valley in which Jamestown was situated was the only attractive area of the island. Ralph Korngold, *The Last Years of Napoleon* (New York, 1959); Frederic Masson, *Napoleon at St. Helena* (Oxford, 1949).

Page 108. THE INDIA COMPANY'S EXPENSE: In 1651 the English East India Company took possession of St. Helena and in 1773 was declared "true and absolute lords and proprietors of the island." When it was decided that it should be the residence of Napoleon in exile the island was garrisoned by regular troops. The governor was nominated by the British Crown and appointed by the company directors. Expenses for Napoleon's residence were shared by the Crown and the company. After Napoleon's death the company resumed full control of the island until it became a Crown colony in 1834. *Encyclopedia Britannica.*

Page 108. THE CHINESE: In 1810 the English East India Company brought Chinese laborers to St. Helena from their factory at Canton.

Page 108. JOS: Could this be Joss, a Chinese image, before which incense was burned?

Page 108. HIS DEATH: Napoleon died May 5, 1821.

Page 108. LONGWOOD: Upon his arrival in October 1815, Napoleon settled temporarily at the Briars, the property of an Englishman, until Longwood was prepared for his residence. He moved into Longwood on December 10, 1815, and remained there until his death. Work was continued on Longwood during the five-and-a-half years of his residence. The Briars could be described as a farmhouse and as "small and inconsiderable." Longwood, however, was a gracious mansion and elegantly furnished. Korngold, *The Last Years of Napoleon*; Masson, *Napoleon at St. Helena.*

Page 110. NEW HOUSE: There is no record of a new house built for Napoleon, or of a house being prepared for him in which he never lived. Dampier seems to have confused the two domiciles of Napoleon. The first house he saw was apparently the Briars, not Longwood.

Page 110. MAD. BERTRAND: This was the wife of Henri Gratien Bertrand. The couple accompanied Napoleon to St. Helena and Bertrand remained one of the emperor's closest and most devoted companions. After Napoleon's death, they returned to France. There does not seem to be confirmation of any intimacy between Madame Bertrand and the exile. The Emperor sometimes walked beside a stream in which two willows were reflected, but he most often confined his walks to the grounds of Longwood. On Bertrand, see *Encyclopedia Britannica.*

Page 110. EXETER CHANGE: The 'Change was a building erected as a sort of bazaar. On the second floor a menagerie was located and wild beast shows were held there. The menagerie was removed from the 'Change in 1828 and the building torn down in 1829. John Timbs, *Curiosities of London* (London, 1885), p. 335.

INDEX